Strategy for the West

Strategy for the West

MARSHAL OF THE ROYAL AIR FORCE SIR JOHN SLESSOR,
G.C.B., D.S.O., M.C.

WILLIAM MORROW AND COMPANY
New York   1954

Grateful acknowledgment is made to Paul Winterton for permission to quote from *Inquest on an Ally* (London, The Cress Press Ltd.); to Walter Lippmann and his publishers, Little, Brown & Company and Atlantic Monthly Press, for permission to quote from *Isolation and Alliances;* to Simon and Schuster, Inc., for permission to quote from *Modern Arms and Free Men,* by Vannevar Bush (copyright 1949 by the Trustees of Vannevar Bush Trust); and to George Kennan and his publishers, The University of Chicago Press, for permission to quote from *American Diplomacy.*

Dedication

To the Bomber Crews of the Royal Air Force and the United States Air Force in World War II who went out and did not return.

Thou therefore, for whom they died, Seek not thine own, but serve as they served. . . .

Contents

Chapter 1. THE REAL WAR   1

I. The strategic object of the Atlantic Alliance.

II. Total war an out-of-date conception—definition of "winning a war."

III. The evolution of war since the eighteenth century—future war general suicide—effect of air power and the weapon of mass destruction.

IV. The Soviet attitude to atomic disarmament—total war has abolished itself—atomic disarmament a disservice to peace.

V. Is there an effective defence—scientifically perhaps possible, but practically not.

VI. World War III in progress now—the prospect before us.

Chapter 2. THE ENEMY   26

I. What we should mean by "negotiate from strength"—the Communist idea of negotiation—what ours should be.

II. Soviet strength—China not in the same category—Russian armed strength—realities and limitations—dangers of overestimating it.

III. Militant communism—subversion in our own countries—Communist exploitation of the "Colonialist Imperialism" slogan abroad—need for Anglo-American unity.

IV. The technique of alternating crises and periods of calm—effect of new tone in Russia after Stalin's death—need to pursue even course.

Chapter 3. THE LONG HAUL   43

I.   The age of coalitions—the principle of balanced force within the coalition—the United Nations Organization —modern diplomacy.

II. The economics of defence in the long haul—impossibility of superimposing new atomic on old conventional strategy—trade with countries behind the Iron Curtain.

III. The defensive aspect of strategy in the long haul—the enemy's advantages—"Thus far and no farther"—the global threat—traditional Russian tactics—the colourbar.

IV. Probability of more "Koreas"—need to isolate and localize—strategy of these small wars—the Yalu "touchline"—action against China—air power an unlimited weapon—other "Koreas" primarily job for land forces.

V.   The offensive in the long haul—economic, political, psychological warfare.

Chapter 4. THE STRENGTH WE NEED   75

I.   The New Look—priorities—first place for the deterrent striking force—but not to be carried to extremes—need for further economies in defence expenditure.

II. Armies—need for strategic reserve in hand—need for forces that can deal with limited commitments by limited means—land force requirement in event of war— modern developments have added to power of defence on land—the pattern of N.A.T.O. land forces—core of mobile armour—the new model "Home Guard" for Germany and other Continental nations—the Territorial Army and National Guard—Civil Defence—am-

phibious and airborne forces—the National Service Act
and the draft.

III. Navies—importance of sea communications—air freight
possibilities—the threat of the mine and the U-boat—
decline since 1943 in capacity of aircraft to combat
U-boat—the great grey ships—economics of naval aviation—lessons of World War II about aircraft carriers
against U-boats and enemy surface shipping—defence
of convoys against air attack—air cover and support for
land operations, the Sixth Fleet—the "Forrestal" class
carriers—conclusion, a few carriers needed for some
time to come—but substantial cuts justifiable—need to
increase mine-sweepers and anti-submarine vessels.

IV. Air power indivisible—the gross extravagance of multiple air forces.

Chapter 5. THE PRIMARY ARM   106

I. Analysis of the presumption that atomic air power is
a decisive instrument.

II. The striking force we need—the "leave it to America"
fallacy—participation of other Allies in the Anglo-
American bomber forces.

III. Air defence—the function of the fighter—conflict between political and military considerations in deter-
mining the force we need—"push-button" warfare not
just round the corner—possible new forms of attack to
be guarded against—other elements of air power.

IV. Battlefield strategy in small wars—some lessons of Korea
misleading—air superiority—ignoring lessons of previous
wars—air can not be effective unless armies are fighting,
lessons of Italian campaign—"austerity" armies less

vulnerable to air action—need to train troops to be tough—need for depth for air action in defence, the advance to and retreat from the Yalu 1950-51—Japan as a main base—nature of bases in future war.

Chapter 6. AIR POWER AND THE PROBLEM OF EUROPE 130

I. German unity the ideal—lack of practical ideas as to how it is to be achieved.

II. Conflict between need for Germany's defence of the West and assurance to France against German domination of Europe—German rearmament—French hesitations—Allied forces not permanently on European soil.

III. The E.D.C.—Dr. Adenauer's policy—possible reorientation of Russian thinking—the dilemma of German unity.

IV. Conditions which any military arrangement must fulfill to be acceptable—Germany can never be a menace again if Britain and U.S. remain determined she shall not be.

V. Various attempted solutions to the European problem —E.D.C.—direct German participation in N.A.T.O.— an American idea—a British suggestion for an extension of the Brussels Treaty to include Germany, the most hopeful basis for a plan.

VI. A scheme based on a revived and extended Brussels Treaty and Sir Winston Churchill's Locarno idea—a new Treaty of Berlin—criticisms and method of application—air control the basis.

POSTSCRIPT 170

Strategy for the West

Chapter 1

The Real War

All are aware that the war potential that either side may mobilize is such as to make another war absolute madness, much more so than the madness which led to the two world wars.

> General Smuts at Cambridge University,
> 11 June 1948.

Indeed, I have sometimes the odd thought that the annihilating character of these agencies may bring an utterly unforeseeable security to mankind. . . . It may be . . . that when the advance of destructive weapons enables everyone to kill everybody else no one will want to kill anyone at all. At any rate it seems pretty safe to say that a war which begins by both sides suffering what they dread most—and that is undoubtedly the case now—is less likely to occur than one which dangles the lurid prizes of former days before ambitious eyes.

> Sir Winston Churchill in the House of Commons,
> 3 November 1953.

I

This is a military appreciation and as such should properly begin with a statement of the object or aim that governs, or should govern, our strategy for the West. First, however, it seems appropriate to define the meaning of the word "strategy" as used in this book. In this second half of the twentieth century that word obviously means something far more than the old simple definition "the art of the general." For the purpose of this study it can be defined as "the management of the political, military, economic and industrial resources of the Western coalition in such a way as to achieve the object of the Free World." From this it follows that the first essential, if our strategy is to be soundly conceived and economically executed, is to be quite clear as to what that object *is* in this struggle with militant communism—what it is that we want to achieve. That may sound obvious to the point of platitude. But in a rather long experience of military appreciations at all levels I have found that the real object is not infrequently overlooked, or at best ill-defined. It is not a thing that can be taken for granted; it should be clearly set out and agreed upon. That is obviously far more difficult in a coalition of free, sovereign states than it used to be in the days when independent national strategies made any sense which, if they ever did, they have long ceased to do. It has been facetiously said that war without allies is bad enough—with allies it is hell! A condition which has made for misunderstanding in the past, and which is not unknown in the Western coalition today, is the acceptance of the assumption that all the Allies are pursuing the same object, whereas some of them have rather different ideas about what in fact we want to achieve.

I shall revert to this later. Meanwhile I suggest, at the risk of some oversimplification, that the object in our strategy for the West is to drive militant communism back behind its own frontiers and keep it there. I know there are difficulties in defining the frontiers of communism, but, though obstinate and formidable, they are, relatively speaking, matters of detail that can be solved. I am aware that this object may sound ambitious because it means to some extent changing the nature of communism; that again I do not believe is insoluble, provided the Free World retains its unity and sense of common purpose, bases its strategy on spiritual values *and* does not try to rush at its object like a bull at a gate. It will not be quickly achieved, but one of our greatest dangers is impatience. There are no short cuts to peace. We are going through one of the greatest secular revolutions of history, and the progress of history is measured not in spasms of five or ten years but in centuries or at least in generations. It may be criticized as paradoxical that an alliance of free peoples whose political philosophy must be assumed to be the Four Freedoms of the Atlantic Charter should be content with this limited definition of our political aims, but great advances are made over a series of limited objectives. To those who believe that each man is his brother's keeper it may appear selfish and feeble; but, however noble our emotions, they are an unstable basis for strategy, which has in this world-wide context to accept its limitations—to deal with mankind as a complex of political entities, not as individuals. We may dislike and despise the crazy philosophy of dialectical materialism; we may loathe the Communist idea of the super-state with its degradation of the dignity of the individual, its denial of the human soul and its paraphernalia of fear and forced labour. But we are quick to react violently against outside interference with our own political systems. And while we may hope that ultimately the Four Freedoms will prevail in all corners of the world and we should work towards that ideal, we are not likely to forward it, but rather the reverse, by forcing the pace. We confuse the issue by talking of human nature as though it were the same in Brixton and Bokhara, in Minneapolis and Moscow, in Paris and Peshawar. It is not; it is very different in these places. But one thing it has in common the world over—among the most universal of human reactions —is a dislike of being dictated to by foreigners. It is not for us to tell other nations what form of government they should have, or try to impose our own political system on Russia or China. As George Kennan has wisely reminded us, "In our relations with the people of Russia it is important, as it has never been important before, for us to recognize that our institutions may not have relevance for people living in other climes and conditions, and that there can be sound structures and forms of government in no way resembling our own and yet not deserving of censure." [1] Democracy is a heady wine, suitable only for seasoned palates. We have only to look round the world today to see the most grotesque absurdities being perpetrated in its name in politically immature countries. For that matter it does not seem to be working as well as all that even in France or Italy. And there is no earthly reason to suppose that the British or American political way of life would suit Russia or China, any more than the French way of life would suit Britain or the American system would be a success in Italy.

So if Russia and China decide to base their systems of government on their own versions of communism (which incidentally are not the same in those two countries and are likely increasingly to diverge) that is no affair of ours. We have no God-given mission to destroy communism. But the converse is equally valid; we in the West are entitled to insist that our systems of government are no business of Russia or China. Communism does become very much our concern when it seeks to dominate other countries, either by external violence—threatened or actual—or by internal subversion, the tactics of the termite. It is then not only legitimate but essential to the preservation of our freedoms that we resist it by every effective means, military

[1] *American Diplomacy* 1900-1950, Univ. of Chicago Press, 1951.

or political. Communism is not a normal political creed like liberalism or socialism, but a conspiracy with the avowed object of destroying political freedom. We may even have voluntarily to surrender a small proportion of our traditional freedom in the interest of the preservation of the rest, but in doing so we are venturing onto dangerous ground and must be especially vigilant lest the cure becomes worse than the disease.

To drive back communism behind its own frontiers and keep it there is not a negative policy of mere containment. It does *not* mean building a sort of Maginot Line of armaments and sitting behind it awaiting attack. It is not a programme for national or international selfishness or social reaction on the one hand nor for short cuts to Utopia on the other. It is no prescription for subversion, corruption and inefficiency in the sacred name of freedom, any more than for intolerance and witch-hunting under the pretext of "security." It does not involve abrogation of responsibility for primitive dependent peoples or surrender to the Communist tactic of exploiting immature nationalism and catchpenny slogans like "liberation of Colonial peoples." And it is not a green light for premature attempts to liberate satellite populations from Communist misrule.

It *does* mean having a liberal, consistent, politically aggressive and *common* policy based on spiritual values, that we are brave enough to pursue because we are strong enough not to fear; a policy that is wise and patient, far-seeing and unselfish enough to prove that the Western way of life is better than the Communist way of life. It means accepting, perhaps for many years, a heavy burden of armaments and not falling for the catch phrase "an armaments race always leads to war"—a parrot phrase that is as meaningless as it is historically baseless. It was not an armaments race that caused the wars of 1870, of 1914 or of 1939. There was no armaments race between North and South Korea or between the real major protagonists in that affair; if there had been, the Northern Communists would not have attacked the South. What does lead to war is when one side does not enter, or drops out of, the race—is so taken up with party politics and sectional interests that it turns its back on reality and drifts into the position in which Britain and France found themselves in 1939, in which foreign policy is powerless for lack of strength to back it.

No one can say how long this present phase of history will last or how it will end, when our object will be achieved and what will be the next stage in the relations between East and West. It may not be as long as we sometimes think, and efforts to relieve tension such as those by Sir Winston Churchill and President Eisenhower should receive all our support. We must be resolute and patient, which does not mean we should be either rash or supine. It is not to suggest that we should merely wait upon events, to envisage the possibility that as butter comes more and more to take the place of guns in the Soviet economy, militant communism as a political theory may become obsolete. However much one may dislike the rulers of Russia, no one can ignore the great progress in the economic and industrial development of that very backward but enormously rich country since the Revolution. In due course, as the standard of living of the Russian peoples approaches that of America—and there seems no material reason why it should not—communism may come to be seen in Russia as the Victorian anachronism that it is in Britain and the United States.

Thus far the object of our strategy has been considered

in relation to the cold war in which we now find ourselves. In what I believe to be the unlikely event that we do not succeed in achieving our object without fighting Russia, then our object in hot war should remain the same as in cold: not to invade or occupy Russia and impose by force our system of government upon her, but to save the world from Muscovite domination, to drive Soviet communism back behind the frontiers of Russia, leaving it to the Russian people among the ruins to draw their own conclusions from calamity and devise for themselves some system of government that will be no longer a menace to their neighbours and a curse to themselves.

II

The massive question facing this generation, the all-pervading doubt that hangs like some sinister smog over the world, is whether or not there will be a third world war, whether our children and grandchildren will have to endure another disaster infinitely more catastrophic and murderous than the two through which we have passed in the last forty years. I believe that, unless the West takes leave of its senses, the answer to that question is "No." I hope, and am optimist enough to believe, that some day there will be real peace, perhaps sooner than we think. But meanwhile the old clear-cut distinction between the states of "war" and "peace" is a thing of the past. At least for some years to come the world will go on, as now, in this sort of curious twilight between war and peace, in which force must have an influence far more permeating than it had in what used to be regarded as normal conditions of "peace," an influence which must be exercised primarily with the object of preventing the outbreak of what we used to understand by "war." Let us here be clear that this does not mean that we should in no circumstances engage in world war. Recent history should be enough to prove that war is never prevented by running away from it. There is all the difference between a policy aimed at *preventing* war and one of which the main preoccupation is to *avoid* war. Britain and France before 1939 tried merely to avoid war, and thereby only made it more certain. There are worse things than physical extinction. To prevent war we must make it unmistakably clear that, while we shall never adopt it as an instrument of policy, we are prepared to fight if our vital interests are threatened, that in the last resort we should not even shrink from striking the first blow as an alternative to bloodless defeat. We have seen too much in our day of the totalitarian technique of the *fait accompli*—the undermining of one vital outpost after another in the belief that civilized peoples are too soft to fight—to cherish still any delusions that war can ultimately be averted by surrender. I believe that as long as that is made clear, and as long as the West maintains the necessary strength to back its policy, total shooting war as we have known it twice in this generation is a thing of the past.

That is a large claim, and to substantiate it I must go back to some first principles, at the risk of being platitudinous. War is basically a conflict of wills. Nations used to embark upon war as an instrument of policy because they wanted someone else to do something, or allow them to do something which they *wanted*, or stop doing something they did not want. It is an old standing cliché that war is a projection of policy, a continuation of diplomacy by other means. It was all part of the same process—you tried to persuade your opponent to conform to your will by a process known as diplomacy; and if that failed, you tried to impose your will on him by force, by a process known as war. In other words at a given critical moment there was a formality called the declaration of war, when you passed from an interchange of diplomatic notes between men in top hats to an interchange of lethal missiles between men in tin hats—all to the same end, the imposition of your *will* upon someone else.

Another obvious truism is that governments did not resort to war unless they thought they had a reasonable chance of winning it. That immediately brings us back to the object in war; *"de quoi s'agit il?"* said old Marshal Foch—"what is it all about?" That great French soldier was the author of another axiom which some of us in the late war forgot, to our cost. He said one must remember that "war is not the supreme aim, because after war there is peace." In the late war Americans were prone to take the far too simple line that the object was just to win, as though war were a football game. I was personally concerned in 1944 with the arguments about strategy in the Balkans and, while some of our American friends shared our views, for the most part their attitude was that in looking to the Balkans and the Middle East, we were taking our eyes off the ball—in the back of their minds they saw us as subtle intriguers, the Red Coats, up to our old Victorian imperialistic games again instead of concentrating on beating the Germans. We see even President Roosevelt at Teheran telling his son that he was not interested in "real or fancied British interests on the European continent. We are at war and our job is to win it as fast as possible, and without adventures." [2] But *why* did we want

[2] Elliott Roosevelt, *As He Saw It*, Duell, Sloan, and Pearce, 1946. It is more generally recognized today that if we had been allowed and helped to undertake these "adventures," the strategy of the West would today have a less unfavourable situation to deal with.

to beat the Germans and win the war? What were we
fighting *for*? What were these "adventures" that President
Roosevelt condemned except measures to try to create the
sort of world we wanted to see *after* the fighting was over?
It was, no doubt, partly this oversimplified conception of
the object in war that led to the calamitous "unconditional surrender" policy announced at Casablanca.

The Americans have learnt a great deal in the last ten
years, and it may not be too much to hope that the true
meaning of winning a war is now universally recognized.
It means not merely forcing an enemy to lay down his
arms and accept terms, but *being successful in creating
world conditions more favourable to yourself than if there
had never been a war*. That ought to be obvious to the
meanest intelligence after the past forty years, and its universal recognition could not be more important, because
on that definition there is not the remotest chance of anyone winning a future world war, and for that reason I do
not believe anyone will resort to it as an instrument of
policy. It is not inconceivable, though I think highly unlikely, that we might stumble into it by mistake or miscalculation. It would still be possible to defeat an enemy
—and the ability of the West to defeat Russia seems to
me beyond question—but no one could possibly create
conditions in the world better for himself than if war had
not been. It is sometimes suggested that the chaos after a
third world war would be an admirable basis for communism; I believe the reverse is the truth and that more
probably there would shamble from the ruins a particularly unpleasant brand of Fascist—from the point of view
of the survivors there would, perhaps, be not much to
choose between the two. The point is, I believe, that the

Russians realize this truth as much as anyone else—after all, they suffered more in the late war than anyone else except possibly Germany. No one can say with certainty that if that were not so we should have found ourselves at war on one of several occasions in the past few years, but I think a realization in the Kremlin of what a third "hot" war would mean was at least a major factor of restraint at the time of the Berlin blockade and of the public adoption by the West of a policy of German rearmament, to say nothing of several occasions during the Korean episode.

III

In assessing the evolution of strategy to this point it is well to look back into history. Without going back too far into the dim ages it can be said, at the cost of some oversimplification, that the recent evolution of war has been on the following general pattern. There were the eighteenth-century wars of *battlefields and sieges*—wars in which armies knocked off and went into winter quarters, "will messieurs the enemy fire first" and all that sort of thing. Napoleon in the nineteenth century made the first relatively modern approach to total war, but even in his day it was war mainly of battlefields and sieges, and, apart from his *levée en masse,* was primarily an affair of professional or mercenary armies. It did not affect the great masses of the populations anything like to the extent of the wars of the first half of the twentieth century. There were exceptions of course; the wretched inhabitants of the Palatinate had the war brought home to them all right. But by and large life in areas away from the battle zones went on very much the same during Jena and Waterloo, Trafalgar and the retreat from Moscow. In England, behind the shield of our sea power, the poor suffered from the high cost of bread resulting from the shutting out of European corn, but otherwise the population as a whole were scarcely affected; Jane Austen's *Persuasion*, for instance, was written during the Napoleonic wars, but the reader would never guess it except for the quite casual reference to Captain Wentworth going "to the wars" and coming home with a nice sum of money in "the funds."

Then, after one hundred years of the Pax Britannica, came 1914-18, a war of *lines*. Erroneously known as World War I, it was not a real world war at all. There were campaigns in the Middle East, in Greece, Turkey and Italy, and great fleet actions at sea. But the main features of that long war were the submarine campaign against British shipping, which brought Britain to the brink of disaster, and the vast siege in France and Belgium at terrible cost in lives and treasure. The air was then too much in its infancy to have any very momentous effect, but 1914-18 did see the early primitive beginnings of direct air attack on centres of population and, for those who had eyes to see, the signs were there. That war had a far greater impact upon the populations than anything that had come before—Britain and France, Germany and Russia paid an appalling toll in lives and material wealth. But it was still a war of battlefields, an affair for soldiers and sailors and airmen, and, except for some starvation in Germany resulting from the blockade, it did not strike direct at the peoples.

The war of 1939-45 was a very different kind of war, a real world war of vast *areas*—Western Europe, the Pacific, Western Russia, North Africa, Southeast Asia—a war of movement. Above all, it was the first air war. For the first time the belligerent countries themselves and their peoples became a primary objective for attack. The cloud of con-

troversy about strategic bombing, the oceans of ink spilt—
no doubt quite sincerely—by those who do not yet understand that they have lived through a revolution in human
affairs, can not obscure the fact that one of the major bel-
ligerents, Japan, surrendered unconditionally with her
armies intact before a single Allied soldier had set foot
on her soil, primarily—not solely, but primarily—owing to
air bombardment, and was brought to the point of that
decision, as we now know, before the first atomic bomb
was dropped. That Germany did not similarly succumb
is little less than a miracle in view of what the German
people suffered. Whether or not we could have enforced
German surrender by air action must always remain a
matter of opinion; my own is that we could certainly have
done so if we had really tried and shaped our policy accordingly. It would take far too long to enumerate here the
various pressures, some of them no doubt unavoidable,
which prevented us from concentrating on the air offensive, and anyway, we fatally prejudiced what even still
might have been a fair chance of success by the crowning
blunder of "unconditional surrender" and later by the
Morgenthau plan. So air power was merely the first decisive
factor among others in Germany's defeat, instead of being
decisive in itself.

In any event the story of 1939-45 contains no more than
a pointer to the future. Even in England during that war
something like normal life went on; the London theatres
were crowded, there was racing at Newmarket and good
cricket at Lords, though matches were sometimes interrupted while players and spectators waited to see whether
a passing V-1 was going to fall on the pitch. We delude
ourselves if we imagine that another great war would bear
the remotest resemblance to the last. The advent of jet-

propulsion, the long-range rocket and the weapon of mass destruction has completely transformed the whole dimension and scope of the problem. It is no use saying that men have thought that before, with the advent of the cross-bow or of gunpowder or of the machine gun; these things merely enhanced the power of men to kill each other on the battlefield, whereas modern air power has made the battlefield irrelevant. It is vain to point to the prolonged resistance of the Germans under the widespread destruction of their cities. Human nature is adaptable and in a totalitarian state can be made to adapt itself to almost anything if it is given time; atomic air power would give no one that time. We are living through a complete revolution in human affairs and at last are reaching the point—which admittedly men have thought before that they were reaching—when war would be general suicide and the end of civilization as we know it.[3] Something, of course, would survive but it would not be recognizable as a tolerably habitable world. We should sink back into another Dark Age.

IV

It is the weapon of mass destruction—the atomic and, in due course, the hydrogen bomb—that has brought us to that point in the evolution of strategy. It is therefore difficult to understand why anyone should be surprised at the Russians' attitude towards atomic warfare. The only

---

[3] It is only fair to point out that an authority from whom I quote freely later in this book, Dr. Vannevar Bush, did not share this view when he wrote his book *Modern Arms and Free Men* in 1949—see for instance page 136 of that book. I do not know whether he would still feel the same after the extraordinary development of destructive agencies, including the hydrogen bomb, in the five years since he wrote. (See Chapter 5, Section I, below.)

really surprising thing is that they should have been so short-sighted as to reject the Baruch Plan in 1947. Apart from that initial inconsistency, which is a measure of their almost pathological antipathy to any form of international inspection and control, they have been perfectly consistent; the use of atomic energy as an instrument of warfare must be outlawed, the production of atomic weapons stopped and all existing stockpiles destroyed, as a condition of any agreement. People who do not agree to that are warmongers. Of course, it is all part of the usual Communist double-talk, but less preposterously irrational than some of the meaningless claptrap that is the stock in trade of Communist propaganda. The argument is perfectly simple: the object of the Kremlin is a Communist world dominated by Moscow; the most effective and sure way of imposing communism on other countries is by the use or threat of the Red Army, the instrument that has brought the whole of Eastern Europe under the Muscovite heel in the last ten years; but as long as atomic air power (and the will on the part of the West to use it if necessary) exists, the Red Army can no longer be used for that amiable purpose without precipitating a third world war of a kind in which Moscow could not possibly gain on balance, whatever the issue; therefore, atomic air power must be eliminated. That is the policy—just as simple as that. The process of putting it into effect is one with which by now we are familiar: work up "peace" campaigns, accuse everyone else of being "warmongers," appeal to the fears of the timid, the wrong-headedness of the cranks, the muddled vanity of ecclesiastical and scientific exhibitionists and the natural decent feelings of simple, kindly people who lack the knowledge on which to base judgment, hire feeble-minded louts to scribble "ban the atom bomb" on walls and put up Mr. Vishinsky to make vitriolic speeches in U.N.O. It is all part of the game, all perfectly logical and, from the Soviet point of view, legitimate tactics. The Kremlin stands to gain by war or the threat of war on the conventional model—or thinks it does; therefore the instrument that has changed the face of war and rendered it fruitless must be abolished. Not a bad indication of some real change in Soviet policy will be when they cease to bang the drum of atomic disarmament on every possible and impossible occasion.

There can be no sane human being who does not long to see the dread of war removed finally from the hearts and minds of men, who does not yearn (in President Eisenhower's words) to find the way by which the miraculous inventiveness of man shall not be dedicated to his death but consecrated to his life. But it never has made and never will make any sense trying to abolish any particular *weapon* of war. What we have to abolish is *war*. Recent history is littered with the ruins of attempts to do that by pacts, leagues, treaties—international agreements of all sorts; none of them ever could or ever can be effective. But what has now happened is that *war has abolished itself* because the atomic and the hydrogen bombs have found their way into the armouries of the world. So the greatest disservice that anyone could possibly do to the cause of peace would be to abolish nuclear armaments on either side. We have in fact found the way to which President Eisenhower pointed us, and at a cost in fissile material diverted to armaments, a sort of insurance premium, which in the long run will be negligible compared to the resources available for peaceable purposes.

Fortunately we can, I think, pretty safely take it for granted that the atomic weapon will not be abolished—

anyway until we arrive at world political conditions which make all weapons, atomic or otherwise, irrelevant and unnecessary. What sense would there be in taking this weapon out of the hands of the soldiers (or rather, out of the hands of the airmen) if we leave in the hands of the soldiers weapons which in two great wars in our day have ravaged the world, and which would leave an almost decisive advantage to that side which has completely ruthless control of its economy and which disposes of vast masses of docile, disciplined and completely expendable manpower? The popular reaction against the atom bomb is not merely revulsion at its destructive capacity; it is a natural emotional reaction to its novelty. Actually the most effective instruments of mass destruction of the late war were the Nazi gas chambers and death camps like Belsen and Buchenwald, and while the military weapon of mass destruction destroyed men's bodies in mass, its political counterpart also destroyed their minds. The Russians perhaps are not quite such experts at that sort of thing as the Nazi butchers, but they have not all that much to learn from them. To abolish the atom bomb would mean, sooner or later, a third world war and quite possibly our defeat in that war; those of us this side of the Iron Curtain who advocate atomic disarmament might stop to consider whether it would profit us to run away from one kind of weapon of mass destruction merely to run into the other. New things are seldom considered coolly and objectively. The tank is now a familiar, conventional weapon; it was the tank that overran vast areas of Europe and was responsible for the deaths of millions and the enslavement of millions more. Yet we hear no voices raised in the U.N.O. demanding the abolition of the tank; no one scribbles "ban the tank" on walls; no—the weapon which must be abolished is the atom bomb, which has neutralized the tank.

So it must be accepted that the atom and the hydrogen bomb have come to stay and that in the unlikely event of another great war they would unquestionably be used. Nothing could be more dangerous than to give the impression to a potential aggressor that we should not use them in the event of aggression. Nothing could suit our enemy better; he would certainly do his best to prevent our using them; he might well preface aggression by declaring publicly that he does not intend to use them unless we use them first, which would present us with a difficult political problem, particularly here in England where we are so vulnerable to this form of attack. It is, therefore, vital that our people should be schooled to recognize this as the specious, tactical opening gambit which is all it would be. They must be educated to understand that the continued existence of atomic weapons gives us an almost certain chance of preventing another world war; that if war did come, atomic weapons would inevitably be used sooner or later, and we should not be prepared yet again to leave the initiative to the aggressor—next time might be one too many; that, on the other hand, the abolition of atomic weapons would put us at a fatal disadvantage vis-à-vis the Russians (to say nothing of the possibility of China being allied against us) in a war that would almost inevitably come in that event; that the one sure defence of Britain lies in the *prevention* of war. There is absolutely no analogy with gas, which both sides had but neither used in the late war. The annihilating, cataclysmic nature of the modern weapon of mass destruction just is not comparable at all to the earlier chemical agents, which in fact were less effective weapons than high explosive and fire;

and by the time the Germans acquired the new, more dangerous gas, we had air superiority over their country and they would have been crazy to launch it.

V

The assumption, or rather, to my mind, the unquestionable fact, that the weapon of mass destruction would be used in any future great war, leads inevitably to the question whether there is any defence against these things. Most of us are familiar with the old cliché that every weapon of offence sooner or later finds its defensive antidote. That may still be true. Personally I do not believe it is. Even against the ordinary manned bomber of today defence would not be easy, but it is not impossible. It is no longer a matter of imposing an attrition rate of 5 per cent or 10 per cent upon a prolonged series of raids until the pace becomes too hot for the attackers to endure as the German air assaults on England and Malta were defeated. Even against distant targets such as those in the United States it must be assumed that the atom-bomb carriers would come, not singly, but interspersed among formations of varying sizes mainly composed of aircraft carrying conventional bombs or radio-countermeasure equipment. And the destructive effect of even one of these modern weapons is so appalling that the task of the defence must be to get almost 100 per cent kill-rate. He would be a rash man who declared that impossible, though we are still some way from it today. But at least not long after we had solved that problem we should be faced with another far more difficult, namely the unmanned bomber —the long-range ground-to-ground guided missile, probably in the form of a two-stage ballistic rocket with an atomic warhead, arriving at two or three times the speed of sound. In these days one hesitates to say that anything is impossible. It may be that the scientist will devise a means of deflecting or prematurely exploding even the 1960 or 1970 version of the V-2. As far as I know, no one today has the least idea how to do it, but it might be done. That, however, is not the real point. Even if it becomes scientifically and technically possible to counter this new form of attack, there then remains the problem of providing the "hardware" and, which might be even more serious, the skilled manpower to operate it. It seems at least extremely unlikely that the new defensive equipment would be simple enough to be operated by the "week-end soldiers" who so efficiently manned the conventional anti-aircraft artillery in the Battle of Britain. There have recently been several scientific investigations into the problem of defending the continental United States against the present possible forms of attack and the estimated cost is understood to have worked out at something between sixteen and twenty-five billion dollars. Let us add to that the cost of providing an equivalent scale of defence for the other countries of the Atlantic Alliance and put the total at, for the sake of argument, twenty-five billion dollars— call it nine billion pounds. And then, just when we have completed that nice little programme, there emerges from some research laboratory somewhere a quite new form of attack which renders the whole thing obsolete, and we have to scrap the lot and start afresh!

In my father's youth there were no motorcars and my grandfather went to school in a stagecoach. To either of them, things which are to us a commonplace today would have appeared as the wildest dreams of a Wells or a Jules Verne. We in our generation must be especially careful not to imagine that we have reached the peak of knowledge and scientific achievement. Our instinct is to deride the idea of gentlemen from another planet, with long blond hair and ski trousers, arriving in America in flying saucers. But is that more inherently improbable than television, supersonic aircraft and the hydrogen bomb would have appeared to young John Slessor jogging along the muddy lanes to Blundells on top of the Sidmouth coach?

Nevertheless in the foreseeable future, which is our concern in strategy for the West, it seems to me to be an inescapable fact that effective over-all defence against forms of attack of which we have already seen the prototypes in action is not a practical economic proposition. That, as I shall later suggest, does not mean that we can afford to ignore defence altogether. It does mean that it would be the height of folly to attempt to cover ourselves every-where—it would be the quickest and surest way to arm ourselves into bankruptcy, than which nothing could suit the Kremlin better. Even in the little island of Great Britain we can not attempt it. In America, even Uncle Sam's pocket is not bottomless and Americans must learn to live dangerously as we on this side of the Atlantic have long since learnt. "Hemisphere defence" just does not make sense, even from a purely selfish American point of view (and if Americans have many faults, selfishness can certainly not be counted among them). America's safety lies in the prevention (again let me emphasize the *prevention* not the *avoidance*) of war, just as does ours; and to allocate to close air defence, on anything approaching the scale which some Americans advocate, the required proportion of the gross national product or the national manpower of America would not only be ineffective in itself, but would inevitably and perhaps fatally prejudice what is known in

Pentagon jargon as the offensive capability that alone and surely can prevent war.

If this is true of the free world, it is equally true of the Communist empire. Great Britain is terribly vulnerable to modern forms of attack, but it has at least one compensating advantage in that it is a small, compact zone to defend. If one considers the vast area over which the cities and vital centres of the Soviet empire are spread (to say nothing of China) it becomes easier to understand why the Soviets should feel they need what seem to us vast numbers of fighter aircraft. In other words, effective over-all defence is just as impracticable for our only potential enemy as it is for the West. Lord Baldwin's dictum "the bomber will always get through" would remain true in another war for at least long enough to inflict mortal damage. There is no reason to be depressed about this. Paradoxically enough, it is the only sure safeguard of peace. If the scientists of the West were to find an effective and economically practicable means of defence, it would only be a matter of time before the Communists did the same—and what then? Why, then air power is cancelled out on either side, and we should be faced with the necessity of matching Russia man for man, tank for tank and escort for U-boat—a pleasant prospect even if we had only to reckon with Russia alone, and one which would be still more formidable if the virtually unlimited manpower and great natural resources of China were in our enemy's camp.

VI

To many this will seem a depressing prospect, a bleak vista of an age in which Eisenhower's two atomic colossi are doomed malevolently to eye each other indefinitely across a trembling world. But we have got to take things as we find them and face realities objectively and without hysteria, not in any mood of fatalistic resignation but with acceptance and with steady nerves. The first of those realities is that there *are* today two colossi separated by an ideological gulf that is not bridgeable by political expedients or written undertakings. But if we accept the truth that war in the sense of total world-wide "shooting" war, has abolished itself through the agency of nuclear and thermo-nuclear energy, then the world can cease to tremble. This is not to make the absurd claim that men will never fight each other again—there will be more small wars—like the settling shocks after a great earthquake; it is to maintain that the Great Deterrent, unless we are fools enough to throw it away, has given us time and the opportunity for the forces of sanity that are at work in the world to assert themselves. The ultimate world peace which is our hearts' desire will not come quickly or easily; "the Parliament of Man, the Federation of the World" will not be born of pacts or treaties or formal international instruments of any kind; it will emerge from a gradual readjustment of the minds of men to the fact that nations or coalitions can no longer impose their will upon others by force of arms. There are the foundations of our strategy for the West—the preservation of the agency that, so long as it exists, has banished total war, and the remoulding of our defence policy on a basis that does not prejudice our chances of winning the real World War III, in which we are now engaged, by preparing for a totally imaginary one.

This is not a programme for eternity. The present state of affairs will not go on forever; it is a phase through which the world must pass, and the tempo of life in this second half of the twentieth century is such that it is unlikely

to last as long as other conflicts of the past which have
had something in common with it, such as that between
Christendom and Islam in Europe. Indeed our task is to
make sure that it does not do so. Measured not in calendar
years or geographical miles but in terms of what man can
do in time and space, human life is so much longer and
the earth so incomparably smaller even than fifty years ago
that we can not and need not tolerate this indefinite con-
tinuance of a condition in human affairs so utterly primeval
in its hates and fears and senseless savagery, its unspeak-
able waste of human life and wealth and happiness in the
Forty Years' War of our time. But we shall not rid the
world of these hates and fears by ignoring them, still less
by aggravating them. If we are determined that the Communist third of the world shall not impose its ideology by
force upon the rest, we must equally accept that we, the
Atlantic coalition, can never impose our philosophy or way
of life upon the rest of the world by the same means. We
can and must reject the Communist idea of "co-existence,"
—which for us would mean the fate of the young lady of
Riga [4]—without insisting that the struggle can end only in
the unconditional surrender of our enemies; that policy
makes as little sense in this present cold war as it did in
the late hot one. Indeed the first thing to realize, if we are
to direct our strategy wisely, is that we are engaged in
World War III *now* and have been for many years. It is
difficult to name a date for its beginning. The uneasy partnership of 1941 to 1945 was not remotely like an alliance;
from the Soviet point of view it was merely a convenient,

[4] There was a young lady of Riga
who went for a ride on a tiger;
they came back from their ride
with the lady inside—
and a smile on the face of the tiger.

and for them extremely fortunate, arrangement which made it possible for them to dispose of one batch of enemies before going on to deal with the others, the rest of the "capitalist" world. For those who like their history neatly paragraphed by dates, a D day for this stage of the war might perhaps be that day in 1948 when poor Jan Masaryk fell to his death from a window in Prague. And the prospect before us is not a sudden flare-up into atomic Armageddon, but the prolonged endurance perhaps for a generation or more of the sort of thing to which we have now become accustomed: an absence of real peace, but an absence also of all-out hostilities on a world-wide scale, coupled with the abandonment of most of the accustomed decencies which in former days used to make international intercourse sound less like the lion house at feeding time.

Chapter 2

The Enemy

Nothing in our age has been more significant than this new technique of aggression and of pacific conquest, which has taken the place of orthodox war.

General Smuts at Cambridge University,
11 June 1948.

I

The statesmen of the West have repeatedly asserted that our policy is to negotiate from strength. Now that we have the strength, or at least have largely remedied the shocking weakness which formerly clogged our policy like a quicksand, we should clear our minds about what we mean by the word "negotiate." For if there is one certainty it is that the Kremlin's interpretation of that word is something quite different to our own. To us in the West it suggests a meeting between two parties with at least some ideas in common as to the sort of result they want to achieve, who are genuinely prepared to compromise to the extent of some degree of give and take, who accept that it will be in the wider interest of both to honour the result of the negotiation, even if it involves some sacrifice or inconvenience to themselves—and who both attach the same meaning to words. There does not seem to me to be the remotest prospect of success for that sort of negotiation with Communists. It is vain to expect normal results from a written treaty with people to whom words mean only what they themselves intend them to mean at the time they are written and bear no relation to normal usage (witness the Soviet use of the words "democratic" and "peace-loving" and the Chinese use of the word "volunteer"), and who have not the faintest intention of honouring any agreement one moment longer than it suits them, who indeed regard written agreements as a perfectly legitimate form of tactics for the ultimate discomfiture of the other party to the negotiations. It is difficult for the ordinary Western mind to grasp that the men of the Kremlin *think* in terms entirely different to our own habits of thought, that with them words are not usually intended to convey thoughts or clarify intentions but more often to conceal and distort them. Let us remember that, as long as the present régime is in power, negotiations will have to be conducted not with true representatives of the common people of Russia, who are no doubt ordinary, simple people like in other countries, but with the Communist clique of party bosses. How can there be any meeting of minds—without which civilized negotiation is foredoomed to failure—with people who in a long series of "treason trials" have given unmistakable evidence of what Charles Morgan has called possessive control of men's minds—"a power to drive a man out of his individuality, to introduce an alien tenant into the house which is his body"? [1] To put it on a more practical basis, how can one expect any sort of respect for normal international agreements from a régime that in the thirty-seven years since the Revolution has shot as spies and traitors, amongst others, all the members of their first Inner Cabinet and all members of the party Politburo

[1] Charles Morgan, *Liberties of the Mind*, Macmillan and Co., 1951.

as constituted after Lenin's death except Stalin, forty-three out of the fifty-three Secretaries of the Central Organization of the Party, seventy out of the eighty members of the Soviet War Council, three out of every five marshals and about 60 per cent of the generals of the Soviet Army?

This does not mean that we should never sit down round a table with the Communists, or that we should never commit the outcome of such a meeting to a written document. There is something to be said for meeting these dictators face to face. We can not deal direct with *peoples* behind the Iron Curtain any more than on this side of it, but they can not be kept by their masters in complete ignorance of what goes on, and inevitably some impression of our purpose and policy must filter through to them. Moreover, that purpose and policy can be put across to their governments, which are composed of men with at least some human characteristics, better by personal contact than by a dreary barrage of diplomatic notes. There is also some advantage in formal written instruments, as long as their scope is limited to specific issues and they clearly involve some interdependent advantage to either side; they serve at least as landmarks and make it anyway less easy and profitable for Communist governments to go back on agreements. It would be a policy of despair to decline ever to meet these men, but in doing so we must be without delusion, must not expect quick or spectacular results—rabbits out of hats—and should borrow something of our opponents' technique of using these meetings as a recognized tactic of political warfare. Nevertheless I think the less we see in the coming years of formal pacts or treaties with the Communist powers, and for that matter between the nations of the Free World, the better. Such

formal agreements as we do undertake should be general
and simple, like the North Atlantic Treaty or the Locarno
Pact; they should not be hedged about with precise conditions which are sure to be interpreted differently with
changing circumstances, and when entered into with Communist governments, should as far as possible not be dependent for their validity upon Communist good faith—
that is, they should be of the nature of formal clarifications
of intention in given circumstances. If we have a consistent
policy rooted in an agreed object and pursue it by flexible
and empirical methods—again borrowing something of the
Communist technique of the *fait accompli*—then gradually it will be borne in upon our adversaries that their
policy is getting them nowhere, and the time may come
when civilized methods of negotiation will again become
practicable and fruitful. We shall never get there by blind-
ing ahead on a programme of unconditional surrender;
our policy must accept that our opponents have their own
rights, hopes and fears. For instance we must take into
account the fear complex that is a perfectly understandable
factor in Russian policy, an attitude of mind developed
over the centuries by a history of invasion by Swedes and
Poles, French and Germans, even by the British in a small
way. Our policy must be a reciprocal programme of "Live
and let live," and the "let live" part of it must apply not
only to ourselves and the enslaved satellites but to the
Russians and Chinese themselves. We must take the quite
new-found opprobrium out of the word "appeasement"
and substitute for the craven submission of the weak its
other, true meaning of pacification and reconciliation by
the strong.

II

We are now passing into a phase of this war in which the chief burden is shifting from the military to the political side. But we have, it may be hoped, at last learnt the lesson that diplomacy, even in its old, more civilized guise and more than ever today, is powerless without force to back it. Not only is freedom from a world shooting war itself dependent on the maintenance of appropriate force to preserve it, but under that shield our strategy in a world that will for some time be far from tranquil and secure requires that we keep at our disposal armed forces appropriate in strength and composition to their commitments. And a major problem is how to do so without imposing a burden upon the manpower and material resources of the Atlantic Alliance heavier than our economy will stand. Therein has lain a weakness of N.A.T.O. up to date—we have tended to think in a military vacuum and dream up astronomical figures of "force requirements" without relating them to the ability of the Alliance to realize them without arming ourselves into bankruptcy. Even the novel experiment of the Three Wise Men and the system of annual reviews have failed to inject realism into the re-armament programme, as they were bound to do because the military thinking on which it was based has not been rooted in realism.

Let us look first with a fresh eye at our major potential enemy—not a bad starting point for any formulation of military policy. A towering reality of world strategy today is the emergence of communism as a world force dominating something like a third of mankind, and the mainspring and motive power of militant communism is the Soviet government of Russia. There are some who see in China a menace as potentially dangerous as the Soviet empire. The New China has unquestionably come to stay as a world power and before many generations are past will almost certainly be the dominant power in Asia. But I believe that to regard China as in any way comparable to Communist Russia as a threat to the Free World is just as unreal as to imagine that she is a mere satellite to Russia. She will be allied with Russia just as long as it suits her, and how long it will suit her will depend very largely on the attitude of the United States and the Commonwealth towards her. She may well be a menace on her own account to British, French and American interests in Asia—how much of a menace will depend largely on our own skill and vision in adapting our trade and colonial policies to the new realities of Asiatic nationalism; but it will certainly not be averted or diminished by pouring good money after bad bolstering a rotten Kuomintang rump in Formosa. But Peking does not share with Moscow the paranoiac pipe dreams of world domination. And we merely confuse the issue by allowing our attitude to China to be governed by emotion rather than reason, thus obscuring the fact that Soviet Russia is public enemy Number One, working implacably against us, world-wide and on every hand everywhere—more often than not by proxy—and pursuing the same aims as the old empire of the Tsars. There is nothing new about Russian behaviour; one has only to read Custine's diary written several hundred years ago to see that the Russian bear has not changed his coat. What is new—and it is an immensely formidable novelty—is that traditional Russian imperialism and expansionism has gained a most dangerous ally in militant communism.

This is no place for a kind of Intelligence estimate of

Russian military strength. We can take it for granted as being extremely formidable. Let us concede the great numbers of divisions, of aircraft, tanks and cannon that are the stock in trade of those who set out to make our flesh creep, admit all the advantages of a centralized economy under rigid authoritarian control, the relatively impenetrable screen of secrecy as opposed to our own extraordinary system of publishing to the world the most intimate details about our military establishments and programmes, and the vast reservoir of acquiescent, brave and hardy manpower. We can agree that the Russians have some good designers and engineers and have produced some excellent weapons such as the Josef Stalin tank and the Mig fighter. It is clear that they have some atomic bombs, though their numbers are probably not yet as formidable as some would have us believe; they have obviously gone further in the direction of producing a thermo-nuclear weapon and sooner than most people thought they would, and it would be folly to assume that they will not produce long-range jet bombers capable of a more serious scale of attack on the United States than the limited one-way "suicide" attacks of which they might be capable today. They have shown themselves to be redoubtable soldiers and have produced some good fighter pilots. And they enjoy what in one sense is a fortunate ability to conduct their affairs in peace and war without sentiment and unhampered by any moral or ethical scruples as we understand them. To face these facts with open eyes is one thing; it is quite another to make out, as some do, that Russia is an irresistible, Herculean colossus, apparently immune to all the military frailties and political handicaps that beset the democracies. I remember many years ago in the 1914-18 war an older officer telling me always to remember that "the enemy is just as

frightened as you are." It is often salutary to take a look
at the situation through the other fellow's eyes, to imagine
for a moment how it may look to the Soviet General Staff.
Experienced military men are familiar with the tendency
that always has to be watched in staff work, to see all our
own difficulties but to credit the enemy with the ability to
do things that we should not dream of attempting. I have
recently heard and read in America quite fantastic estimates of the present Russian ability to damage the United
States. It must be admitted that the American system
whereby defence appropriations have to be justified before
Congressional committees lends itself to the dangers of
overstatement. And the British tendency to underrate our
enemies is apt to excite an exaggerated reaction in discussion with Americans. But if it is dangerous to underrate
our enemy, it is equally so to overrate him. We must preserve a sense of proportion in these matters. Constantly
to exaggerate the danger depresses public morale and in-
duces an unhealthy nervous condition among the people,
and if carried to extremes leads to irresistible demands for
unwise expenditure and critically affects our strategic freedom of action. At the end of 1941 Mr. Churchill, restive
under the still repeated warnings of the possibility of invasion of England, insisted that a properly qualified team
be appointed—with all the necessary information and staff
assistance—to produce *as Germans* a plan for the invasion
of England. I was the Air Force member of that team and
after six weeks' hard work, interrupted by the excitement
of Pearl Harbor, we produced a voluminous plan, which
we submitted under a covering note saying, in effect, that
it was a rotten plan and we did not think it would succeed,
but it was the best we could do. That was the last we heard
of the invasion bogey. An exercise on those lines might be

profitable today. No one denies that in another great war even in the near future the United States would be attacked from the air and suffer some serious damage. But when it is suggested, as I have heard it said, that the United States could be knocked out as the arsenal of the North Atlantic Alliance, then, writing as one who has been concerned for a good many years with air bombardment planning, I beg leave to say that it is nonsense. As time goes on the danger will increase until, as I have suggested, a great war would be almost as suicidal for the United States as for Russia. Meanwhile do not let us be distracted by geopolitical talk about heartlands, which was all very well in Mackinder's day but ceased to be relevant with the advent of the long-range bomber. Russia's central position has some tactical advantages, vis-à-vis her neighbours, but in a world air war she would be at a decisive disadvantage. Air power has turned the vast spaces that were her prime defence against Napoleon and Hindenburg and Hitler into a source of weakness. In these days of near-sonic speeds, the depth of penetration necessary to reach some of her vital centres is offset by the size of the area to be defended and the fact that it can be attacked from almost all round the compass. Compared to that, a team of experienced planners, with resources estimated on a generous but not unrealistic scale, assigned to plan as Russians to knock out the United States, would find themselves faced with a hopeless task. Both countries are vulnerable, but Russia far more so. In the ultimate future both sides might suffer mortal damage in such a war. But therein lies the security of the Atlantic coalition, not in any craven cumulation of purely defensive resources that can have no direct impact upon the enemy.

In the sphere of military strength on land the Soviets have still great superiority, not only in numbers but in other important respects such as battle-readiness and the ratio of firepower to numbers of men. That will probably always be so; indeed it would be fatal for the Atlantic powers to attempt to match Russia in this field. Even there the Soviets have their difficulties. Logistic problems, such as fuel supply in the field, are formidable enough in defence and hardly bear thinking about in the deep penetration into enemy territory which is so lightheartedly envisaged for the Red Army and Air Force. And the forces of the old Austro-Hungarian Empire thirty-five years ago would not be the last to suffer from the disintegrating effect of large dissident minorities—the satellites might well be a source of serious weakness to their Soviet overlords. Relatively, the Red Army is far less overwhelmingly superior than it was even three short years ago. There was a time when there was virtually nothing to stop the forces normally stationed in the Soviet zone of Germany from walking almost unhindered to the Channel coast and the Pyrenees. It would be a very different matter today. Not only are the forces under S.H.A.P.E. stronger, better equipped, better organized and trained and endowed with high morale, but also their sphere of land warfare is the one in which the nuclear weapon has given advantage to the defender. It may be true that the Western armies could do no more than hold the line of the Rhine or the Elbe. But the point is that the old temptation to an enemy to exploit an easy success is gone. He could drive us back, but it would be a tough, stubborn and lengthy business, more than ever when the German forces take their place—as they must—in Saceur's order of battle. And, though we should not yet be content with the existing land and air forces of N.A.T.O. in Europe, we should only weaken ourselves if we aimed higher than that. The issues of peace and war, and the outcome of another great war should it come, will not be decided by the armies.

III

But far the most potent weapon in the Soviet armoury is militant communism. It is too simple a half-truth to say that it has owed its success to the backing of superior military force. It is a dynamic doctrine which has an especial appeal to the discontented and the uprooted and those who like to have their thinking done for them, but which is not confined to the uneducated and ignorant. It is no good our building the strongest ramparts against attack from without if our defences are sapped by the insidious infiltration of the enemy in the disguise of international-ism, anti-militarism and freedom for the underdog—all, no doubt, excellent things in themselves but the direct antithesis of what communism really stands for. Whittaker Chambers, the ex-Communist of the Alger Hiss affair, who can be assumed to know what he is talking about, has this to say about it: "What communism has done is to make the morality of war its permanent single standard by which it always lives and acts—such an evil thing has never before happened on such a scale in human history. . . . [It is] a militant and semi-military faith engaged in a war, now open, now concealed, against all others. . . . [The Communist] is simply the soldier, in uniform or business suit, whom you or your children have faced or will face in one form or another, in military or civil combat." [2] It is a particularly difficult enemy for the free world to counter, just because the free world *is* free, and freedom of thought and speech is one of our essential articles of faith. Neverthe-

[2] From an article in *Look* magazine.

less, though it is true that there is not much to choose between the red shirt of communism and the brown one of nazism, it is silly to pretend that there is only a knife edge between flabby tolerance of subversion and disloyalty, and the blatant oppression that is fascism; it is perfectly possible to take appropriate democratic action to preserve our freedoms from the putrefaction of Marxist-Leninism without swerving to the infantile intolerance of McCarthyism. The first essential is to recognize this attack for what it is; to distinguish liberty of thought from licence to distort other peoples' thoughts; to take positive action, on lines which have been so successful in Sweden to counter the notorious influence of communism in key trade unions and as the fomenter of unofficial strikes; to counter communism in education, in which the first step is to recognize the obvious truth that teaching is one of the most vitally important professions and reward it accordingly. We in Britain must realize that we have achieved a social revolution in our time, and that it is now up to us, if we wish to continue to enjoy its fruits, to consolidate our gains. If we persist in trying to get more out of the kitty than we put into it, we shall merely be playing our enemy's game and proving that the Communist is right when he asserts that the Western way of life is foredoomed to failure.

In the wider world sphere it is sometimes less easy to identify the real enemy; there is, for instance, such a thing as genuine nationalism which, while it often has all the faults of immaturity and runs into channels that we deplore with results that are inconvenient for us, should be distinguished from communism. But the real enemy constantly fertilizes and exploits this sort of thing and feeds on its results. And here is room for closer and more sympathetic understanding between Americans and British.

That wise observer Walter Lippmann has said of the old out-dated rôle of the United States as an auxiliary, a source of aid to its European friends and not, as now, the major partner in the coalition of free peoples, "It allowed us the luxury of standing apart from our principal allies, particularly from Great Britain and France which had direct interests and commitments all over the world. Standing apart, we could support them and we could refuse to support them, we could approve and we could criticize what they did. We could measure all claims on our support, particularly in the colonial and dependent areas of Asia and the Middle East, by our own ideological standards." [3] These are luxuries in which it is dangerous to indulge today. It is surely time that more Americans outgrew the outlook on colonialism of which a typical but unusually unfortunate manifestation was Mr. Roosevelt's attitude at Yalta. Experience is a good school, and perhaps their dealings with Mr. Syngman Rhee may help Americans to realize that gentlemen like the Mullah Kashani and Major Salah Salem have not as much in common as they are sometimes led to believe with the Founding Fathers of the Republic. The policy of undermining the position of Britain and France in the Middle East and in colonial territories is part of the original Bolshevik programme inspired by Lenin himself, and we do no service to Anglo-American relations by ignoring the fact that it still receives powerful nourishment from the traditional American concept that there is something basically vicious and immoral about colonialism in general and British colonialism in particular. British friends of America realize that the history of America as a nation begins with a revolt against colonial rule, and understand the distrust

[3] Walter Lippmann, *Isolation and Alliances: An American Speaks to the British*, Little, Brown and Company, 1952.

of authority that stems from 1776, but they feel it might be more generally recognized that the government of Queen Elizabeth and Sir Winston Churchill is not that of George III and Lord North. And they may perhaps be excused if they sometimes wonder why, when American troops cross a narrow stretch of fresh water called the Nueces River and the United States acquires Texas, New Mexico, Arizona, Utah, Nevada and California, that is manifest destiny laying a golden egg—the fulfilment of the American dream; [4] but when British troops cross a wide stretch of salt water called, say, the Indian Ocean and Britain acquires Ceylon or Malaya, that is colonial imperialism and as such reprehensible and immoral, a denial of the rights of man. Let our American friends—and for that matter those British Babbitts of the Left [5] to whom the rebel and the terrorist are always right and the British colonial administrator always wrong—face the fact that "leagues against imperialism" and "liberation" of colonial peoples are openly acknowledged tactics of Soviet communism. The thinly disguised satisfaction with which so many organs of the American press still hail each and every symptom of the so-called "disintegration" of the British Empire encourages our common enemy and does grave disservice to our essential unity. In the interest of that unity and the common effort, which are essential if we are to defeat not only our common enemy but the real enemy of the less politically mature peoples of the Free World, let them bring their thinking up to date and acknowledge that premature self-government for such peoples is very

[4] James Truslow Adams, *The Epic of America*, Little, Brown and Co., 1931.
[5] Arthur Koestler's phrase.

liable merely to open the door to communism, as we have
recently seen in British Guiana.

IV

Our adversary's object remains a Communist world dominated by Moscow, a world in which all the countries are
run for the benefit of Russia by Communist stooges and
puppets subserviently taking their orders from the hard-
headed oligarchy in the Kremlin. It is the task of our generation to convince them that that is a phantasm, and instead to lead the way to a world in which nations mind
their own business, including the business of normal, decent international intercourse in the political, economic and
social spheres—Ernest Bevin's ideal of being able to go
anywhere without a passport. We can not do that by force;
nor can we do it without force. It will call for the utmost
patience, wisdom and foresight as well as for courage and
firmness—the highest qualities of statesmanship. But the
men we are dealing with for the time being—and we need
not imagine they are the permanent masters of Russia—
understand nothing but strength, and these qualities will
be fruitless unless they are backed by the necessary strength
and the courage to use it if and when that becomes essential. Keeping our object clear before our eyes, which is the
first essential of any strategy, our strategy for the West
must be to go steadily ahead towards that goal, accepting
the necessary hardships and sacrifices for as long as may be
necessary (and they are not so intolerable as all that) and
not swerving off at a tangent after any hare that jumps up.
We must not allow ourselves to be lulled into apathy by
periods of apparent calm nor panicked into intemperate
action by apparent crises. We shall probably have plenty

of both but, like Kipling's Triumph and Disaster, should "treat those two impostors just the same," understanding that they are all part of the game—tactical moves by which the enemy tries to achieve his object, which is the antithesis of ours. The nonsensical vapourings about so-called "preventive war" on the part of those for whom talk is a substitute for thought, which reached their peak when the danger appeared greatest and of which we have fortunately heard less of late, are no more irrational than the reaction of large sections of the public in some democratic countries to the hints of a New Look in Soviet policy after the death of Stalin. The many wise and important things that Sir Winston Churchill said in his great speech in the House of Commons on 11 May 1953 were obscured by a sort of smoke screen of muddled, wishful thinking generated by his suggestion for a high-level meeting between the leading powers. By all means let us be on the look-out for the first signs of any real change of heart, and be ready to go to meet them halfway; the attainment of our object involves a change of heart, and we shall never attain it if we close our minds to any approaches short of complete surrender. But do not let us mistake tactics for strategy. And if, whenever some Soviet spokesman in the Kremlin or the United Nations behaves for once with less than their usual insufferable rudeness and contumacy, we are going to throw in the sponge and say N.A.T.O. is unnecessary and we must not be beastly to the Russians, what hope is there for any consistent strategy? That is hardly an exaggeration of the state of at least large sections of public opinion in some European countries in the summer of 1953; it was not unknown even in Britain and the United States. It was well described as being like what happens when one side in a tug of war suddenly lets go of the rope, the other side falls flat on its back in a jumble of arms and legs. It is to be hoped that more recent exchanges have induced a more rational frame of mind. But the point is that this sort of tactics will be used again; we are in for a long, hard period of difficulty and some tension in the relations between East and West, a period in which it will be more than ever important to observe the old Roman axiom "rebus in arduis aequam servare mentem." A test of the self-discipline and common sense of the democracies, in which if they fail they are probably doomed, will be their ability to sustain the virility of the Alliance and endure the necessary sacrifices to maintain their strength during long periods of decreasing tension, when their danger is less immediate and obvious than in the conditions which called it into being.

No one should underrate our enemy in this bleak, cold war of the mind. He is formidable, ruthless and without scruple. On the main essentials of our strategy there can be no compromise. He is our enemy as long as he continues to impose his tyranny through his quislings and professional butchers on the historic nations of Eastern Europe, arms and nourishes civil war and rebellion in the more backward countries, treason and subversion in our own. But equally let us not overrate him. He may be a colossus, but he has feet of clay. President Roosevelt once said, "The only thing we have to fear is fear itself." That is as true today as ever it was, and to that saying we need add only one word—"disunity."

Chapter 3

The Long Haul

It has fallen to our generation to fight yet again, and on a world scale, the age old duel between tyranny and freedom. That is the heart of the struggle between the Soviet Union and the West.

Paul Winterton, *Inquest on an Ally.*

I

True unity among the nations of the Free World, the voluntary subordination of national policy to a common international policy and purpose as opposed to the artificial, monolithic tyranny of the Soviet system, is today a *sine qua non* of survival. Isolationism—"going it alone" or whatever idiotic description may be applied to it—is just another way of spelling defeat in detail. No nation, not even the United States or U.S.S.R., can today pursue an individual, independent strategy of its own. There is no such thing as a national strategy—actually it has made no sense for many years and the disasters of 1939-40 were largely due to our blindness to that fact. The age of great coalitions in which we live is partly the natural result of the extraordinary shrinkage in the size of the world due to modern methods of transport and intercommunication. But it is also due to the nature of modern war itself. Another great war even more than the last would be real world war, a war of continents between two conflicting creeds far more fundamentally antagonistic than Christendom and Islam in the Middle Ages. In such a war there would be no neutrals; neutralism today is another form of escapism, the attitude of the ostrich. This is not to say that every nation in the world however small and wherever situated should today choose between full partnership in one or other of the two great military coalitions. There are valid practical reasons, for instance, why some of Russia's smaller neighbours should not be in N.A.T.O. For others, the sort of limited membership of the Atlantic club implicit in their refusal to allow Allied bases on their soil, though unwise, is understandable; they are in effect banking on the ability of their more powerful Allies to protect them by preventing war and are doing so, presumably, in the knowledge that if that fails, their inability to pay their full subscription, so to speak, would mean that they could not enjoy the full advantages of membership, in that in the event of war their security would be less assured. Elsewhere a somewhat self-righteous attitude of impartiality is more unrealistic. In some Asiatic countries it is due partly to a perhaps understandable reaction to their new-found independence of Western authority—a sort of growing pain of adolescence as nations—and partly to the fear that if they got embroiled they could not be defended against more powerful neighbours. It may not make sense, but it has to be accepted as one of the facts of life, and incidentally one of the handicaps that the Free World has to endure because it *is* free. Those of us who do face realities and act in unison to avert the world-wide common danger have to carry some passengers who enjoy the pleasures of the voyage without working their passage. That is unfortunate, but it can not be helped; we obviously can not put pressure on anyone to join the Alliance. And a danger against which we must be specially on our guard is that of the cold war becoming one between the white West and the coloured East—with Russia as, at best, the *tertius gaudens*.

No people should imagine, however, that if another great war should come they could stand aside, watch the two protagonists batter each other to pieces and profit from the result. Even if they did succeed in remaining uninvolved to the extent of not having to endure the "red-hot rake of war" upon their own soil, they would in the long run share the fate of the rest of civilization, in greater or lesser degree. And it is a fallacy to suppose that any free nation can pull its full weight in the world or have any real freedom of action outside the coalition of the free peoples, still more that it can effectively influence for good or ill the policy of either camp. Switzerland traditionally and India more recently at Panmunjon have demonstrated the advantage of having some uncommitted third party as long as that is possible. But if it really came to the ultimate issue, then not even Switzerland could expect to be immune from the effects of what would indeed be Armageddon.

Meanwhile we have in N.A.T.O. a grand alliance of a kind unprecedented in history, which makes all comparisons of the situation today with that in earlier phases of this world crisis of the twentieth century quite unrealistic. It is not in itself complete as a global coalition against the world-wide threat, and to try to extend its commitments would be to subject it to an unbearable strain. We must have other groupings of a similar but not identical kind, inspired by the same common purpose and linked together by some common membership—primarily that of the three

"Standing Group" powers. We have already the Anzus Pact. And it should be our aim to supplement that by, or expand it into, a more comprehensive Far East-Southeast Asia Group, not necessarily on the exact model of N.A.T.O., but of a nature not only to contain Communist aggression in the political and military fields, but to coordinate and direct those positive, constructive measures of economic and social development that are the essential counteroffensive against communism. Some day also—it may be hoped before it is too late—certain Middle Eastern States may come to their senses sufficiently to play the honourable part which was designed for them in the Middle East Defence Organization, rejected by a former government of Egypt but essential to complete the grand alliance and to restore stability and hence prosperity to a part of the world whose prime necessity they are. In this context again unity and concerted action between the English-speaking peoples is especially important. The Asiatic is not slow to seek advantage by playing off one party against another, and a dangerous source of friction would be the growth of an impression that America is using her economic strength to acquire the influence that Britain has surrendered, an impression which we may as well admit has not been entirely without justification in recent history.

If this great coalition is to stand firm it calls for two things—or perhaps it would be more accurate to say two manifestations of the same thing, surrender in the common interest of some degree of national sovereignty. On the part of the major partners, the Great Powers, it calls for patience, tact and understanding, a willingness to bear a disproportionate share of the burden, and resistance to the sometimes natural inclination to thump the table and use their power to impose their views upon unwilling partners. In this lies one of the weaknesses of the Soviet system, while in N.A.T.O. the Great Powers have so far done pretty well in this respect, and it has not always been easy. For the smaller partners it calls for a more realistic and less parochial view than some of them have sometimes taken. Small nations with no world-wide responsibilities should, for instance, think twice before shaking a donnish finger at "colonialism." [1] I have heard representatives from more than one such European country talking as though there were something reprehensible about British resistance to communism in Malaya, apparently ignoring not only that this is merely another front in the same world war, but also that Malaya, as Britain's best dollar-earner, is a major factor in our ability to bear a much larger share of the burden of N.A.T.O. than some of our critics. Nor is it reasonable that smaller partners should behave as though no danger spot on the other side of the world can be any concern of theirs. They must take the rough with the smooth and realize that they depend for their security upon being part of a coalition, and there are no part-time partners in a coalition. If World War III of the popular concept did break out, they would be in it whether they liked it or not and whether it broke out in Berlin or in Turkey, on the Elbe or on the Mekong. Strategy today is world strategy and it is no more possible to shape it merely to suit the limited interest of one particular country than it is to confine a typhoon to a potato patch. On the part of all the

[1] It was not an Englishman but a German who has recently written, "It seems strange that so few people in England (or indeed on the Continent) realize that in the Far East the Union Jack does not fly for Britain alone. Were it to be hauled down for good one day, it would mean the end for France and Italy, for Norway and Portugal as well as for Britain in that part of the World." (P. Grubbe in *The European Review*, December 1953.) To that it is probably true to add that it would also be the end for the United States in that part of the world.

partners, the preservation of the Alliance requires that we curb the senseless "anti-each-otherism" that today must cause such solid satisfaction to the Politburo, and may become a real menace if it continues unchecked. Americans must not expect to be loved (we British were not loved when we were the strongest and richest power on earth), but they are entitled to respect and, if not gratitude—for gratitude unfortunately has never been a conspicuous influence in international relations—at least appreciation of the generously enlightened self-interest that inspired Lend-lease, the Baruch Plan, Marshall aid and the North Atlantic Treaty. Their partners equally are entitled to sympathetic understanding of their problems and perhaps to the recognition that America's foreign relations would be happier if they were rather less at the mercy of internal politics.

In a coalition true economy of effort should involve the principle first invoked, I think, by General Omar Bradley in his speech in Chicago in 1949, of properly balanced forces *within the coalition as a whole*—each partner contributing what his national resources and characteristics and experience best fit him to contribute and not each trying to reproduce within the Alliance a sort of miniature microcosm of the whole. This principle could only be applied to a limited extent, if at all, to the few Great Powers with world responsibilities, but unfortunately it has proved in practice extraordinarily difficult to apply at all. All sorts of political prejudices and traditions, vested interests and national prides come into play. And one may look around him today and see several examples of small nations trying, quite vainly, to have their own army, navy and air force all complete as though there were no such thing as N.A.T.O. in existence. That is the antithesis of the sound strategic principles of co-operation and economy of force, and some day we may learn to think really internationally in this respect, but it looks as though we may have to put up with the antithesis for some time to come.

There are some who are impatient of military alliances and yearn for the creation of a world police force to maintain the rule of law between the nations. We can share their aspirations without agreeing that anything on these lines is anything but a pipe dream in the present state of the world. The history of the Military Staff Committee of the United Nations Organization should be enough to prove that a world police force is a chimera without a world government—the political horse must come before the military cart. We must be patient enough to work towards our goal by limited advances. It would be folly to scrap U.N.O. or try to turn it into an anti-Communist organization, which would amount to the same thing; there is a tendency, particularly in the United States, to swing from one extreme of exaggerated faith in it to the other of contemptuous dislike. We must do our utmost to make it work, but again by the method of limited advances, and should not be cynical or despondent about it on the one hand or, on the other, blind to its shortcomings and disadvantages which are many, especially from the point of view of the Great Powers. Britain perhaps more than anyone else has good reason to know them. We have sound grounds for impatience when small, remote member states with no world responsibilities, whose own system of government would not be tolerated for a moment in any British territory, indulge in the pleasures of throwing stones at our colonial administration in the glass house of the Trusteeship Council. And the sad tale of Abadan was an example of how our adherence to U.N.O. has made it virtually impossible to deal in the old-fashioned way with people like

Dr. Mossadegh, while affording us no compensating protection for our interests. Such people can in U.N.O. enjoy all the pleasures of power without responsibility, all the privileges of the U.N.O. system while rejecting its obligations, openly flouting the Hague Court and making a shameful nonsense of the principles of decent international dealings on which the system was intended to be based. Nevertheless, while recognizing that the majority of the member states are still too politically immature to enable the system to work in the way it was designed to work, let us not condemn U.N.O. out of hand as a talking shop. There are advantages even in a talking shop; it is a safety valve and sounding board, and it is an educative process. We must learn to put up with the behaviour of the Russians and their stooges, and of the Mossadeghs of this world, and trust that experience and the passage of time will teach them to behave like civilized human beings. Actually the organization, and its sub-organizations in a dozen different spheres are doing a great deal of useful if inconspicuous work. If we expect too much of U.N.O. in its infancy we shall only subject it to a strain which it is still too immature to endure. We for our part could do more to make it work. We can decline to allow anybody to "shoot his way into the Security Council" without indefinitely refusing to admit Great Powers into U.N.O. because they have Communist governments—that is no more tenable than the attitude of Russia indefinitely banning nations like Italy or Ceylon. U.N.O. is not a conservative club; it is a world organization and it takes all sorts to make a world. So, while consolidating and extending the less comprehensive coalitions upon which the security of an imperfect world must in our time depend, let us regard them as a limited but none the less vitally important step towards the system of world government with its international police force, into which perhaps U.N.O. will develop some day.

Meanwhile I suppose it is too much to hope for a return to the elementary decencies and time-honoured procedure of international intercourse that used to be known as diplomacy, including a reasonable measure of secrecy while negotiations are actually in progress. "Open covenants . . . openly arrived at" seems to be another way of spelling open disagreements openly aggravated, and the history of so-called open diplomacy, from the Palais Rose to Panmunjon, may excuse a nostalgic sigh for striped pants and discreet silences. But if Communists are to be induced to use international negotiations as anything but subversive propaganda designed to make agreement impossible, that would involve some reticence and self-denial on the part of politicians and the press this side of the Iron Curtain. Diplomacy can be nothing but a farce when every move in the game from the opening gambit is blazoned in headlines, taken out of its context, misunderstood and misrepresented and garbled on platforms and front pages on both sides of the Atlantic and the Channel.

II

"If we are going to fire a missile at the enemy," writes Dr. Vannevar Bush, the principal defence scientific adviser to the U.S. government in the late war, "we should be very sure before we devote a large amount of manpower and materials to it that it is going to harm the enemy more than it harms us, that the damage it causes will interfere with his ability to continue the struggle more than it costs us from the same point of view." [2] If that is true of what we used to know as war, it is more than ever so of this present cold war. It is a truth which we may as well admit we have tended to overlook in our N.A.T.O. planning. When the nature of the crisis between East and West became really apparent to us with the open aggression in Korea, it was perhaps inevitable, and indeed right, that the democracies, who had done after 1945 what they always did after all their wars and jeopardized the peace they had paid so much to win by throwing away the weapons with which they had won it, should rebuild their strength regardless of expense. The well-merited sense of urgency at the time, the justifiable haste with which the rearmament programmes were undertaken after Dean Acheson's grave invocation at the Brussels meeting of the Atlantic Council in December 1950, undoubtedly led to some underestimation of the costs involved, and the military can hardly be blamed for failing to foresee the economic effects of the Korean war and the meteoric rise in costs that to some extent stultified the original programmes. Now that our military strength is so largely restored, the danger less immediately menacing and our measure of the economic climate more informed, it is essential that we should reassess our military requirements to accord more closely with the prospect before us, which is not a sort of modernized version of World War II in the near future but the "long haul" under the wings of atomic air power. We have to satisfy ourselves, in fact, not only that Dr. Bush's missile is the right sort of missile but that it is likely to hurt the enemy, if we have to fire it, more than it hurts us to make and get ready to fire if necessary.

We British suffer here from the condition that for the

[2] *Modern Arms and Free Men*, Simon and Schuster, 1949.

past forty years the sort of forces required for major war and for our minor military commitments in time of peace have been steadily diverging. In my youth they were to all intents and purposes identical. For our minor wars on the Indian frontier, in Africa, etc., we used "horse, foot and guns," and in 1914 we went to the first great war of this century with horse, foot and guns. That was obviously a very convenient and economical state of affairs, but since 1914 it has been slowly but steadily becoming an anachronism. To-day, although for many of our British cold war commitments the foot soldier with his personal arms and light supporting weapons is still the major requirement, for major war we want something quite different. Unfortunately the age of air power does not justify the abolition of land forces. Not only can we not yet be absolutely certain that we shall not stumble into total war by accident or miscalculation, but also the prevention of war in itself requires that we be ready to wage it and we could not wage it without any land forces. For this reason alone (and there are others) we must have armies suitably equipped and armed to fight against a highly organized and heavily armed enemy, and the arms and equipment for this purpose are highly complicated, suffer a rapid rate of obsolescence owing to the modern tempo of scientific research and development and, partly for that reason, are enormously expensive, far more so than the equipment required for what in our unregenerate days we used to call "imperial policing."

That, no doubt, is a condition which is less embarrassing to others among our Allies. But for one and all it is true that we can not ignore the economics of defence. To arm ourselves into bankruptcy would be to accept self-imposed defeat. No one minds enduring the utmost material hardship for a time, when we are fighting with our backs to the wall. But when the prospect before us is a generation or more of armed vigilance, we are deluding ourselves if we imagine we can permanently allocate to armaments a proportion of the gross national product comparable to that which, whether we like it or not, we have to spend when we are actually fighting. We are now at a strategic crossroads—the point of decision in the most revolutionary period of transition in the history of war—and we have got to choose one road or another. It might to some appear logical and prudent to stick to the road of traditional strategy and the conventional means to carry it through—the massed divisions and wings of the original N.A.T.O. concept, or rather of the old Western Union concept as taken over and elaborated by N.A.T.O. It would not be wise, because even now we can see far enough down that road to perceive that we could not in fact provide enough conventional force in the state of readiness and with the necessary reserves to match the Red Army, even with the support of the atomic weapon on the battlefield, without incurring the self-defeat of economic ruin. One thing is clear beyond doubt: we can no longer afford the attempt to superimpose the new atomic air strategy on top of the old conventional strategy. So we have not really a free choice of roads, but must and fortunately can make a virtue of necessity. We must maintain atomic air power to prevent war; we must therefore depend upon it—and we can safely—as the primary agent for the defeat of our enemy if the deterrent fails, and we must supplement and support it by conventional forces, organized, equipped and trained on really modern lines and with all the assistance that science can give them, but of a size and cost that the free nations can afford to maintain without breaking themselves.

A realistic appreciation of the economics of defence in-

volves an adult approach to the thorny problem of trade
with Communist countries. It is not really a very intricate
problem if it is measured objectively by the same yardstick as Dr. Bush's missile—will it harm the Communist
countries or the Free World more if we decline to trade
with them? If on balance it pays us to trade with countries
behind the Iron Curtain, generally or in any specific field,
then we should be silly not to do so. It is idiotic to refuse
to trade with someone just because you do not like him,
as President Eisenhower has himself pointed out. We may
dislike the idea of dealing in goods produced by slave
labour, but to refuse on those grounds does not benefit
the slaves or bring them nearer to freedom—rather the reverse. Irritation, however well-provoked, is not a substitute
for a policy, and economic force, like military force, should
be used not in a mood of "blind petulance" but for "rational and restricted purposes rather than for purposes
which are emotional" in George Kennan's words.[3] No one
suggests that any member of the Alliance should profit by
supplying Red China or any other Communist state with
the sinews of war, and if the people who throw that sort
of accusation at their allies do not know it is a lie, they
should not insult the free air with their prejudiced ignorance. The agreement of the British government of the
day to release the Nene jet engine to Russia was unfortunate and I thought at the time it was a mistake, but it
must be judged in the light of international relations as
they existed, or as we in Britain and the United States mis-
takenly saw them, at the time it was done and not in the
bleak context of the cold war. Anyway, since that date we
British have loyally observed our international agreements
not to supply strategic materials to Iron Curtain countries;

[3] *American Diplomacy* 1900-1950, Univ. of Chicago Press, 1951.

long before the United Nations resolution on the subject we had cut off supply of strategic materials to Red China, and indeed we have taken a lead in setting up and operating the machinery for applying these strategic controls. Britain lives by her export trade and that alone enables her to play her part as America's major partner in N.A.T.O., yet we have seriously injured it by a strictly conscientious interpretation of the term "strategic material." It is, however, senseless to expect us to refuse all trade with Communist countries merely because we dislike their governments. No one in Britain blames America for allowing Japan under MacArthur's proconsulate to trade with Communist China; indeed the sooner we all realize that China is a literally vital area for Japanese trade, very much the better for us all. No sensible person in Britain thinks any worse of the U.S. government for buying tungsten from China while American "boys" were fighting Chinese "volunteers" in Korea; indeed we should have thought it merely silly of them not to do so if China had the tungsten and they wanted it to help their war effort, and if it was *more in their interest than that of China to do so*. In the long haul that lies before us we must behave like grown-up people and not silly schoolboys, and trade with whom we wish if it is to our advantage to do so. Actually East-West trade may have less economic importance than is sometimes suggested. But it is reasonable to hope that it will help gradually to break down the log jam; it can do no harm and may do good to the subject peoples under Soviet domination and may be an important factor in leading to more normal international relations. Anyway, we should always apply to it the acid test of common sense self-interest—does it on balance benefit us at least as much if not more than our opponents in the cold war?

III

Mere containment is an unsatisfying business, but all strategy has its defensive side and the nature of this new war is such that the initiative inevitably lies in large degree with our adversary. That is a disadvantage as serious in cold war as in hot, but it is one which is inherent in the nature of the struggle and we must make the best of it and consolidate our defences while neglecting no opportunities (and they are many) to take the initiative. It would be entirely misleading to describe our policy and purpose as being no more than the preservation of the *status quo*, but we are inevitably on the defensive. As General Smuts put it, "the peoples of Western Europe have built up a culture and civilized way of life and thought which forms the proudest and most precious achievement of man, and remains a standard for the rest of the world to repair to and advance under." [4] That standard is fundamental to the Free World and we are bound to preserve it; the Communists are its implacable opponents and seek only to destroy it. To that extent the initiative rests with them and we are on the defensive, though obviously the achievement of our object demands far more than merely covering ourselves, boxing with our right arm only. I have already mentioned some handicaps under which the Free World suffers just because it is free, and there are others which we must also face and overcome because we can not avoid them and remain true to our standard. The Communists will always have more opportunities than we to fight their war by proxy, at relatively low cost to themselves in treasure or human life, not that they care much about human suffer-

4 Cambridge University speech, 1948.

ing. Their standard of international morality, or lack of it, gives them what from their point of view is a legitimate weapon in the fifth column, while blandly protesting the monstrosity of interference in other peoples' affairs. Perhaps our most dangerous weakness is that our idea of freedom includes—rightly or wrongly but anyway unavoidably —liberty for a people to frame their constitution and conduct their government so inefficiently as at least to run a grave risk of indigenous Communist parties getting voted into power with, of course, the active support of the Cominform. These be formidable dangers which can only be overcome by facing the reality of them. But they are not mortal, and the disadvantages are not all on our side—far from it. There is enough evidence from behind the Iron Curtain to give us confidence that if we believe in the validity of spiritual values and act up to our principles, we can look forward to seeing our way of life prevail over this other philosophy which is rotten at the core, based as it is on the denial, not only of the Christian ethic and all civilized mankind's intrinsic instincts, but of almost everything that distinguishes man from the beasts. If that sort of thing prevails it will be our fault and we shall have deserved our destruction. It will not be easy. We lost a terrible lot of ground in the years after the fighting stopped before our eyes were opened to the realities of Soviet policy. It will take us a long time to recover from the disastrous misjudgments of Teheran and Yalta, and we are still in the defensive phase of the new war. But more recently we have not done so badly. It is barely six years since General Smuts said at Cambridge, "the great task before the world today is the salving of Europe, materially, politically and spiritually. Beside it all other tasks and problems shrink into comparative insignificance." We delude ourselves if we imagine that task is completed. But the European scene has been transformed since he spoke, and the events of June 1953 and the elections in Germany demonstrated that the Kremlin has lost a crucial campaign in the most important theatre. In Asia and Africa the enemy still batters on our gates. But we should not allow the sordid squabbles at Panmunjon or the Alice in Wonderland absurdities of Syngman Rhee to obscure the fact that the record in Korea can show one major victory. Said Smuts in 1948, "The hour has struck to call a halt to this fifth column in its advance to the West, and to say to the great power behind it in clear and unmistakable terms: thus far and no farther." If President Truman had no other claim to fame, he would go down in history as the first man to say just that, and to back his words by force. It is perhaps too soon to measure the end effect of his action, but it is surely at least a partial explanation of the recent setback to communism in Persia. Other peoples this side of the Iron Curtain have seen that the Kremlin has been served notice, in the only unmistakable terms, that if it oversteps the mark it will be met with force.[5]

The setbacks to Soviet communism in the European theatre should contain for us a warning. This menace of militant communism is a global danger and we must treat it as such. In a world where political and economic circumstances change so rapidly and unpredictably, it would be folly to assume that because the threat took a certain form and direction yesterday it is necessarily the same today. Our strategy must be flexible and the main emphasis in our defensive policy should be adapted to meet the changing threat. Soviet communism has several characteristics in

[5] It was not fear of Russian intervention that prevented the British sending troops to Abadan.

common with Tsarist imperialism—the basic nature of Russian policy has not fundamentally changed—and one is the tactical withdrawal in the face of determined opposition, *reculer pour mieux sauter*—finding themselves stopped here, draw back and have another try somewhere else. Sir Charles Petrie, the famous historian, has written, "Ever since the reign of Peter the Great at the beginning of the eighteenth century there have been three avenues of expansion open to Russia—that is to say Europe, the Middle East and the Far East. Whenever she has found one of these avenues closed to her she has tried another one, and it is difficult to resist the conclusion that this is what she is doing today." [6] Checked by Britain and France in the Crimea, the Russians turned to Central Asia, from there back to the Balkans until again they found their ambitions in the direction of the Mediterranean blocked by Great Britain, then back eastwards again, this time to China and the control of Manchuria, till their defeat by Japan in 1905 switched their attentions back to Southeast Europe and the troubled waters of the Balkans once again. May it not be that the Kremlin has decided that it is up against something too tough in Europe and so, while keeping up the smoke screen there, is putting on the heat, as usual by proxy, in Asia? It was, I think, Lenin who said that the road to Paris lay through Peking and Delhi. We must not allow all our attention and too much of our strength to be contained by a show of force in Europe while the real attack comes round a relatively open flank in Asia, a flank where the bastion of Allied solidarity in Europe is still not matched by corresponding unity or strength. Petrie implies that that is happening and further suggests that since the

[6] In the *Daily Mail*, 17 December 1953.

failure to absorb the whole of Korea, the Kremlin may be following its usual tactic and turning to the vacuum left by the decline of British influence and power in the Middle East. In spite of the setback represented by the fall of Mossadegh and his Tudeh stooges, Communist activity in the Middle East and the recent Muscovite flirtations with the military revolutionary junta in Egypt lend some support to that suggestion.

One of the less spurious appeals that Soviet communism has for politically immature peoples is the theoretical and to a large extent the genuine absence of the colour bar from Soviet practice. This is a reproach which the Free World must face and eliminate if our strategy for the West is to be effective on the long term. An attitude of anachronistic hedonism towards the colour problem is not peculiar to the so-called "colonial imperialists." Actually the British have set many examples of progressive liberalism in this field, and colour prejudice is seen at its worst in many parts of the United States. Nor is it all one-sided; there are in some Asiatic countries men who profess and call themselves democratic statesmen who talk as though their aim were to turn the cold war into one between coloured and white. I know it is easy enough to say this and more difficult to put it into practice, but when we say we stand for the four freedoms and the dignity of the individual man with a soul of his own, we must mean it—the individual *man* not the individual *white man*—and act up to it. This is not a plea for the immediate imposition of self-determination and self-government upon primitive, naked peoples with about as much idea of the meaning of democracy as Neanderthal man. Nothing can be more senseless or destructive of the true happiness and prosperity of these simple savages, as we must fear we shall soon see as a re-

sult of the recent sorry farce in the Sudan. It may be unduly
pessimistic to assume that all is lost in the Sudan, that the
fruits of fifty years of the best administration in British
colonial history will necessarily go up in smoke. The danger
of this grossly premature grant of so-called "freedom" to
the Sudan lies in its possible effects on the rest of Africa.
The Free World can not afford to sit by and watch the
almost limitless resources of that great continent go the
way of some parts of Asia. It is vital that we should check
the spread of communism in a vast area whose potential
wealth is in most respects greater than that of the United
States. In British colonial Africa we have little to be
ashamed and much to be proud of, and we deserve from
our English-speaking Allies and fellow-subjects in the Commonwealth sympathetic understanding and assistance and
not ghoulish satisfaction at our setbacks. They must understand that we do not intend to allow the fruits of decent
government to be eaten away by subversion and disorder
which, if not initiated by communism, is always fostered
and supported by it, that we shall deal with it by force
when necessary as we are doing in Kenya, and that this inevitably makes claims upon our military strength.

But equally we have no intention of allowing these setbacks to deflect us from our purpose of orderly political
development in colonial Africa. The development of self-
government in the Gold Coast may be a bit premature,
but it is a liberal and forward-looking experiment which
will be followed elsewhere. In East and Central Africa we
have to solve a problem which as far as I know has never
yet been solved satisfactorily,[7] that of a free multi-racial
community living in harmony. That should be a challenge

[7] I suppose New Zealand could be quoted as an example, but the problem there is far less complex and difficult than in Africa.

and inspiration to British genius, and one of the most encouraging signs of recent times was the overwhelming victory of the Federal party in the first elections in the Federation of Rhodesia and Nyasaland, on a policy of equal opportunity regardless of race and colour. It is a sign of strength too that, in spite of Mau Mau, that same policy has been publicly adopted by the European Elected Members in Kenya. The unity that is an indispensable element in our strategy for the West must be unity, not only between white men, but between all, regardless of colour, who stand for the culture and civilized way of life and thought that stems originally from ancient Greece.

No one can write a primer of defence in cold war. Keeping our strategic object clearly in our mind we must deal with situations as they arise, foreseeing them when possible and no longer allowing one outpost of the Free World to fall after another without a shot being fired, until our main defensive position is hopelessly compromised. We have lost too much to that technique already in the days of our weakness. We need lose no more—we have not now that utterly defenceless feeling that led to the surrender at Munich and which some of us recalled unpleasantly clearly three or four years ago. We may see no more of the well-known technique of infiltration and the outrageous *fait accompli*, perpetrated in the knowledge of our reluctance to embark on full scale war, but we must be ready to resist it if they try it on again. If a policy of active defensive containment was sound in Greece, so it will be elsewhere if it becomes necessary. But we have gone a long way since Greece. Our adversary respects force and knows that we have it; we should leave him in no doubt that we should use it if necessary. Do not let us worry too much about being provocative—I do not mean we should trail our coats—and we should remember that, in George Kennan's phrase, the Kremlin "can be placed by tactless and threatening gestures in a position where it cannot afford to yield even though this might be dictated by its sense of realism." [8] But if the Russians wanted war, they would not worry about waiting to be provoked, and we should not allow our strategy to be deflected by weak-kneed fear of provoking them, or refrain from the use of force, on a scale necessary to preserve a vital interest against attack by force, for fear of it leading to general war.

"Only morons talk lightly of war in an atomic age. Russia will do nothing to start a general war as long as the West is strong and united. Only by the narrowest of margins did she survive the German attack. There is no possibility that she will deliberately challenge the combined power of the United States and the British Commonwealth and the rest of the democracies." [9] Those words may have been unduly bold at the time they were written six years ago, though they have been borne out by events. They are certainly true today.

IV

That, as I have already said, does not mean we have seen the end of fighting—no such luck. In the spring of 1948 I suggested in a lecture to the officers of the U.S. Air University that we might be entering upon an era of "Crimean" wars—relatively small, localized affairs. That suggestion may not sound as foolish today as no doubt it did at the time, because since then we have seen one such war, in Korea. I think this generation may well see more "Koreas" else-

[8] *American Diplomacy 1900-1950*, Univ. of Chicago Press, 1951.
[9] Paul Winterton, *Inquest on an Ally*, The Cresset Press, London, 1948.

where in the world and we should not shrink from them, any more than we did in June 1950. Our action then has undoubtedly made a repetition less likely to be necessary. But if the free peoples could accept all that sacrifice and face those risks for a point of principle in an area which intrinsically is of relatively slight strategic importance, why should they hesitate to do it again in an area which might be really vital to them? It is true that in Korea Russian troops were not openly engaged, but it is to be hoped that the courage of the free peoples is not equal only to resisting the puppets of Russia. The difference is not one of principle, and if we are going to run away because Russian troops and not merely their stooges attack our outposts, for fear of provoking major war, then not only would that be the best way of ensuring another great war, but also the first step to losing it.

No one can be absolutely certain that another outbreak of fighting elsewhere would not flare up into world war though I think it is unlikely. These minor wars of the future, the other "Koreas," if they come, should be regarded as what they will be, tactical episodes in the real world war of our time, which it will be in our interest to isolate and keep localized, as unquestionably it was in Korea. This will call for strong nerves and cool heads, for very wise, patient handling—not too easy in the democracies, where international policy is always to some extent at the mercy of press and politicians in some election or Cabinet crisis or Congressional investigation somewhere or other. This will not be the only disadvantage under which we shall suffer, and we may as well face it; it will always be easier and less expensive for the totalitarian dictatorships to fight this sort of war than for free peoples. That does not mean they will be victorious, any more than they were in Korea. But unconditional surrender may well be no more attainable as the seal of victory without disastrous results in a small war than it was in a big one. And we certainly should not achieve our object by deliberately blowing up a small localized campaign into World War III. The impatience of Americans over Korea was very understandable; they bore the brunt of the cost and the casualties, and they may well have to do so again in similar circumstances. But they should preserve a sense of proportion about these things. For generations Great Britain had to maintain thousands of troops overseas and suffered heavy casualties in many small wars. Ah, but, I can hear American friends saying, that was a different thing—those were the old imperialist wars. Perhaps—but they might note that ill-wishers of America today describe the United States as the new imperialists; *plus ça change, plus c'est la même chose.* The casualties on either side even in the modern small war are a drop in the bucket compared to the holocaust of life that would be another great war; they do not really look so terrible when compared even with the annual toll of life on the roads in civilized countries. Anyway, the real point is that we must keep our object squarely in view and be quite clear about what we are fighting *for*, what result we want to flow from any contemplated course of action—what its long term, wider implications will be, however immediately attractive it may appear. We should beware of the democratic tendency against which George Kennan has warned us, in a passage from which I have already quoted, whereby our attitude to the fighting "lies less in any objective understanding of the wider issues involved than in a profound irritation over the fact that other people have finally provoked us to the point where we had no alternative but to take up arms. This lends to the democratic war effort a basically punitive note, rather than one of expediency." [10] Finally we should remember that there are very seldom short cuts in any sort of war; it's no good getting impatient and making the disease much worse in a desperate effort to cure it. Any action must always be subjected to two acid tests—will it pay us tactically and will it achieve the strategic result we want from it?

By isolating these outbreaks and keeping them localized I do not mean that we should allow them to drag on and drain our strength indefinitely. We might have to take very drastic action—more than we did in Korea. There is no basic reason why we should not use atomic weapons, subject only to the two acid tests to which I have just referred. Nor in another Korea need there necessarily be another Yalu, another sort of touchline over which the ball is out of play for us but in play for our enemies. One can not draw a blueprint for these hypothetical future campaigns, can not say definitely in advance, this or that should or should not be done; it will entirely depend on the circumstances at the time and whether it will help to achieve our object or not. The United Nations airmen deserve the highest credit for their discipline and forbearance in the almost intolerable conditions of the Yalu touchline. They had to refrain from crossing it because, in spite of the obvious tactical disadvantages of abstention, strategically on balance it paid us not to. We heard at the time a great deal of talk about the handicaps under which we suffered by being precluded from bombing airfields, depots and communications north of the Yalu. But we for our part enjoyed an

[10] *American Diplomacy 1900-1950*, Univ. of Chicago Press, 1951.

extraordinary artificial air superiority and a complete immunity not only from air but submarine and mine attack on our own airfields and depots and communications which, with the ports, were far more vulnerable than those of the enemy, who anyway did not require great truck convoys to move his stores and ammunition. In other words, this curious restriction on tactical freedom happened to suit *both sides* very well in the circumstances of that campaign. If it is argued that United Nations air action against Communist objectives over the river would not have meant retaliation in kind, I can only beg to disagree. I think the evidence that it would have meant just that was at least as strong as the evidence that led me to believe that the Chinese would in fact intervene, as they said they would, if we advanced to the Yalu on the ground.

I mention this only as illustration of the strategic principles that I have suggested should govern our actions in any future small war. For the same reason I think it worth referring to the opinion, held by many sincere and intelligent people, that once China had been branded by the United Nations as an aggressor, we should have instituted a naval blockade and bombed the inland communications and depots through which supplies reached the Communist armies in Korea. I believe we were perfectly right not to do that, not out of any emotional regard or sympathy for China, but for two perfectly good strategic reasons. First, it would not have been tactically effective. It was not the slightest use accepting all the effort and risks involved in a naval blockade—including the need to hold up Soviet flag ships and prevent the use at least of Port Arthur and Dairen as well as Chinese ports proper—unless the blockade was going to be effective in preventing or interfering with the flow of essential supplies to Korea. There

was no reason whatever to imagine that Chinese depend-
ence on seaborne imports was such that it would do anything of the kind. Similarly, I know of no evidence to show
that to bomb railways and depots in China, on the scale
that we could then afford to divert to that task, would
have interfered seriously with supply to the Communist
front, when the constant bombardment of the few railways
in Korea itself failed to do so. Secondly, there were sound
reasons of strategic policy against doing anything of the
kind, which might or might not have decided the issue had
there been reason to suppose it would be effective on tactical grounds. We were operating in Korea as agents of the
United Nations; so far from winning the war in Korea,
action on the lines advocated might very well have spread
it. It might have been a different matter if we had been
prepared to launch total war against China using the atom
bomb, but were we? [11] Had we in the conditions of 1950
the strength to spare from other commitments? What
would have been the effect on the rest of Asia, and on our
world strategy as a whole? These are the sort of questions
one has to ask himself. It does not necessarily follow that
the answers would be the same in a different sort of circumstances. It is merely an example of the need in *all* circumstances to ask old Foch's question *"de quoi s'agit il?"*
—"what is the object?"—and shape our course accordingly.

I shall revert in a later chapter to some lessons of Korea,

[11] "In the controversy last spring between General MacArthur and the
chiefs of staff, the deciding reason for limiting the war to the Korean
peninsula, for not expanding it into China, was that American strategic
air power is not only committed to the defence of the Atlantic community,
but that it cannot as a matter of technical procedure be employed except
with the full and willing collaboration of Great Britain and France."
Walter Lippmann, *Isolation and Alliances: An American Speaks to the
British*, Little, Brown and Company, 1952.

Actually, this quotation may give a rather too simple impression. There
were other strong reasons.

but there is one other point appropriate to this brief sketch of some strategic principles that may be relevant in any future small war. People who are always on the look-out for grounds for denigrating air power claim that it was ineffective in Korea, because the Communists were able to sustain their resistance in spite of our enormously superior air strength. The truth is that it was far from ineffective; in my view there were times when the United Nations armies would very likely have been pushed into the sea had it not been for our air power. But it was not decisive, and it will not be decisive in any other small war in the future, and for the same reason. These little wars will be what I understand old Clausewitz called "limited wars"; air power in its fullest sense is an *unlimited* instrument. In Korea it was limited, in my view rightly so, in the objectives it was allowed to attack and the weapons it was allowed to use. I think it will be similarly limited in any future small war—in fact that condition is inherent in the very term "small war," but if air power were really given its head the war would not remain "small." So these Koreas of the future will again be mainly a job for the land forces with air cover and support of all kinds, and we must not assume that another time we should again enjoy the immunity from enemy air attack that we did in Korea. The real strategic function of the air in these small wars will be to keep them small, to hold the ring and prevent them spreading by the threat of the big stick in the background.

V

These violent episodes, however, will be the exception; they may not even happen at all. There may be no more than rebellions—though they can be violent enough in all conscience, as the deadly toll of French life in Indo-China has proved. It may be that we are approaching a negotiated peace there on terms that the Free World could accept. But if that does not happen, few things could be more important than that the French and their associated states should be given all possible aid, if necessary by armed force, to quell the Communist rebellion in Indo-China and stabilize that vital front in Asia.

The offensive in this new war must mainly be one of ideas. And, as I have said in an earlier chapter, our vital task is to prove that the Western way of life is better than the Communist way of life. "If we can show that the Communist predictions are wrong and that capitalism can develop and change without breakdown, if we can build better than the Communists and provide security and prosperity without destroying freedom, then the Communist parties will retreat, their cause will decay and the foundations of Soviet power will begin to crumble." [12] That task, that strategy, must cover an area far wider than the confines of the Atlantic Treaty powers themselves. It is a world-wide strategy of two main fronts, economic and political, closely connected and supplemented by a vigorous and imaginative offensive in the field of ideas, what we know as psychological warfare. On the economic front in Europe we have made a splendid start; the Marshall Plan was the "Overlord" of the new war, though we are still far short of the new V.E. day. We have yet to match that in the undeveloped countries of Asia and Africa, though much is being done, and the Colombo Plan and the Four Point policy show that at least our tactical theory is sound. Our objective must be to provide economic elbow room

[12] Paul Winterton, *Inquest on an Ally*, The Cresset Press, London, 1948.

for backward peoples to develop freely on their own lines, and in particular to ensure adequate food supplies for the increasing populations in Asia, where one tractor and one technician are worth a hundred in the West.

The economic offensive must be matched by the political one, of which the objective, long term though it may be, should be the Soviets' weakest point, the satellite states and in particular the most vulnerable of them, Eastern Germany. The events of June 1953 show how shallow-based is Russia's control there. We should not be caught napping again as we were then and should be quicker to exploit our opportunities. That does not mean we should set out here and now to liberate the satellites. It is both too late and too soon for that. We ought to have thought of it before throwing away our strength in the popular rush to "get the boys home"; it is too soon because, just as in the last war it was our experience that psychological warfare was of little avail unless it could be quickly supported by military action, so in the cold war the psychological offensive must be backed by practical, effective political and economic action.

Nevertheless, the psychological offensive if it is well directed, with limited objectives that can be supported, will be of high importance and value. "The long-term world struggle will be fought out mainly in the minds of men. For us, many of the weapons of peace lie unexploited. Certainly we must deal forcefully with force, but we shall gain more in the long run by dealing truthfully with falsehood. The West has nothing to conceal and not very much to be ashamed of. Let us start with a total war of facts." [13] We have not done too badly in this regard—the foreign service of the B.B.C. in particular, with its strictly factual treat-

[13] *Ibid.*

ment and its avoidance of blatantly open propaganda. This business requires very careful handling—it must be done in an adult way; if it is conducted crudely in an amateur way and laid on too thick, it does more harm than good. The real essential is that it must be based on a positive, common policy—all its agencies must be tuned in to one wave length, the object we want to achieve. But psychological warfare is more than mere propaganda. It can be conducted by other means. Its tactics should be to drive a wedge between the Communist minority and the non-Communist majority and then between those "national" Communists who are not prepared completely to subordinate their countries to the Kremlin and the other more faithful stooges of Moscow—Lenin's tactics in reverse. Other peoples should be encouraged as the time ripens to follow the example of Yugoslavia. And the possibilities inherent in the support of political by economic action, such as outbidding Russia in the supply of raw materials and the provision of machinery and technicians, are only one reason for a common sense, objective attitude to trade with countries under Communist rule.

But the real offensive in this new war is in the field of foreign policy and diplomacy in their fullest sense, the art of the statesman and the business of the foreign ministries and state departments of the Free World; in the advance and stabilization of economic prosperity and the gradual spread of political unity this side of the Iron Curtain, on the pattern set by the European Coal and Steel Community; in the conquest of want and ignorance in the backward countries of Asia and Africa, and the development of their vast resources for the common good; and in the patient but persistent intensification of pressure, whenever and wherever opportunity offers, to free the satellite states from the yoke of Moscow, until at long last the Iron Curtain is rolled up and the Russian peoples themselves can become equal members of a free community of nations.

As the motto for that great endeavour, what could be better than these words of one of the very few really great men of our day: "Let us across the long centuries reaffirm Pericles's great slogan for democracy—'Happiness is freedom and freedom is courage.' " [14]

[14] General Smuts.

Chapter 4

The Strength We Need

No foreign policy can have validity if there is no adequate force behind it and no national readiness to make the necessary sacrifices to produce that force.

Sir Winston Churchill, The Gathering Storm.

For good or ill, air mastery is today the supreme expression of military power, and fleets and armies, however necessary, must accept a subordinate rank.

Sir Winston Churchill, Speech at Boston, Mass., 1949.

I

It is customary in democratic countries to deplore expenditure on armaments as conflicting with the requirements of the social services. There is a tendency to forget that the most important social service that a government can do for its people is to keep them alive and free. However much we may regret the need still to maintain great military establishments, as a sad reflection on the sanity of mankind after the two appalling disasters of the past forty years, to ignore that need is to blind ourselves to the facts of life, and in fact very few people beyond the lunatic fringe now do so. Where, until recently, there has not been any such measure of unanimity is in the problem of what type of forces we require and in what proportions the defence budgets should be allocated between the different arms. It would be too much to claim that there is as yet general agreement on that score, but lately there has been in both Britain and the United States a nearer approach to it, largely under the pressure of economic stringency, and a growing recognition that to try to go along on traditional lines—the so-called "balanced forces" theory which really amounts to little more than a rather unimaginative share-out, cutting up the cake into more or less equal slices for each of the three armed services—can only lead to a standing arms bill which is beyond our capacity to sustain, particularly in the long haul that lies before us.

If the theme that has been developed in the earlier chapters of this book is accepted, that problem automatically falls into proper perspective. It is all a question of priorities, not of "overriding priority," a term that makes little practical sense, but of putting first things first. It is quite certain that none of us, not even the United States, can afford to maintain all the forces that can quite fairly be represented as more than desirable. The question we all have to answer is whether they are vital in the literal sense of the word, accepting the truth that if we try to be strong everywhere we shall be strong enough nowhere. Having cleared our minds on our policy, stated our object and agreed on the basic fundamentals of our strategy for the West, we must have adequate strength—not necessarily ideal nor vastly superior to any potential enemy, but adequate—in what Sir Winston Churchill has described as the supreme expression of military power. And the kernel of air power is the bomber—today the long-range, jet-propelled high-altitude bomber with its skilled crew; tomorrow perhaps the long-range controlled missile. Britain and the United States must maintain as long as may be necessary, as a first charge on our military resources, that force which is the Great Deterrent, the real preventive of war, the only force which, if the deterrent should fail, can bring instantaneously overwhelming pressure to bear on aggression at its source.

It is very seldom wise to carry things to their logical conclusions, and the airmen can no doubt rely upon their comrades of the older services to assist them in resisting that temptation. No one service can meet our commitments in cold war and no sensible airman has ever suggested that air power could defeat an enemy unaided or even ensure our survival without the co-operation of the other arms. The fact that the Pax Atlantica today rests as squarely on the Anglo-American bomber force as did the Pax Britannica upon the British battle fleet [1] for a century before 1914, no more means we can get by with nothing but bombers today than that the British Empire could have been content with nothing but battleships in the nineteenth century. But the fact must be faced that if we are to restrict our defence expenditures to within tolerable limits, some economies will have to be found within our military establishments. These establishments have a knack of growing a good deal of surplus fat. That perhaps is inevitable in time of war and it takes time to sweat it off when the fighting is over. It is liable to grow again in crises of near-war when the financial stringency normal to times of peace has rightly to be relaxed. There is no room for surplus fat today. In the United States a revision of the

[1] Walter Lippmann has reminded us (*U.S. Foreign Policy*, Little, Brown and Co., 1943) that most Americans have never heard of the fact that the Monroe Doctrine of 1823 was preceded and given validity by an understanding with Canning, the British Foreign Minister of the day, that Britain and the Royal Navy would support the United States in their policy of resistance to further European encroachment in the Western Hemisphere.

defence budget for the financial year 1954 imposed, mainly upon one of the three U.S. services and without fatal results, a reduction in the sum earlier considered necessary amounting to something not far short of the total defence estimates in the United Kingdom for 1954. There is little doubt that a similarly drastic operation could be performed in other directions without tragically affecting the fighting efficiency of the other U.S. services. In Britain unfortunately the surgeon's knife has already done its worst as far as fat is concerned. (Incidentally, even allowing for differences in costs and in U.S. standards compared to British, Americans might with advantage borrow some of our technique of producing good fighting units on what they would describe as a shoestring). There can, however, be little doubt that in Britain, and I believe that it will eventually be the same in the United States, some more savings will have to be found by effecting actual reductions in fighting potential in other spheres—in all three services—in order to maintain the essential level of technical efficiency and battle-readiness in the air striking force.[2] Similarly we can already see that the hitherto accepted programmes of other N.A.T.O. powers will have to be scaled down, and we may hope that in that process more regard will be given to the principle of balanced force within the coalition (to which I have referred in a previous chapter) and less to the quite understandable but in these days prohibitive luxury of historical tradition and service pride. It boils down to what I have said earlier, that we can no longer afford to superimpose the new atomic air strategy on top of the old conventional strategy of armies on the early twentieth-century continental scale with their great supporting air forces.

[2] This was written before President Eisenhower's Budget Message of 21 January 1954.

We must cut our coat according to our cloth and can count ourselves fortunate that the new garment, while it may lack some of the cut and colour of the old, can protect us from cold and wet at least as well, and indeed better.

II

To say that we can not afford Continental armies on the scale hitherto envisaged for N.A.T.O. unfortunately does not mean that we can look forward to a reduction in the number of regular divisions now under arms, anyway in the near future. On the contrary, the numbers and fighting efficiency of the land forces of some members of the Alliance still require some increment. It should be, and indeed is, our aim to liquidate as far as possible the outlying commitments in which so many of our land forces are at present deeply engaged, such as Korea, the Middle East and Indo-China—replacing them with indigenous troops— so that we can regain that strategic freedom of action which only an uncommitted reserve under our hand can afford us. The success of the United States in raising native divisions in the Republic of Korea shows how valuable these indigenous forces can be; our admiration of that success, and of the qualities of the Korean troops, need not obscure the fact that for generations the British have set an example in the organization and training of local forces, as the excellent armies of India and Pakistan today bear witness. The U.S. government announced in January their intention to withdraw two divisions from Korea, and President Eisenhower, in his State of the Union Message to Congress, laid down as one of the principles to govern U.S. defence planning, that "our armed forces must regain maximum mobility of action. Our strategic reserves must

be centrally placed and readily deployable to meet sudden
aggression against ourselves and our allies." For France a
solution of the war in Indo-China, where such a great proportion of her best regular manpower is contained (and
such a tragic number killed) by one of the typical Communist diversionary movements, is important not only in
itself but also to restore the traditional strength and battle-
worthiness of the French Metropolitan Army, or to enable
the French to take the lead which they should take in the
Army of the European Defence Community if it materializes. We in Britain would be deluding ourselves if we
imagine that the release of the divisions now tied up in
the Suez Canal zone will mean that we can effect great
economies by disbanding them. Seldom in history has the
central strategic reserve been reduced to such skeleton proportions; it is not long since the regular infantry in the
United Kingdom were down to the essential minimum
Household troops for duty in London. Even today, out of
just under twelve regular divisions, no less than eleven are
overseas, including our superb armoured contingent of
three armoured divisions under the orders of the supreme
commander in Europe. And the fact that we were com-
pelled in 1953 to send regular infantry to prevent Com-
munist-inspired disorder in British Guiana of all places, is
only another example added to Malaya and Mau Mau of
the essential need to have an adequate reserve in hand.
Moreover, if I am right in thinking that we may see more
"Koreas" in our generation and that they will call primarily for the action of land forces, that surely disposes
of any idea that we can safely look forward to substantial
reductions in our regular armies, at least until world political conditions are far more stable than they seem likely
to be in the immediately foreseeable future.

The fact is that air power, as I have already said, is in its fullest sense an unlimited instrument, and must be supplemented by forces of the type that can deal with what are, or should be, limited commitments by limited means. Air power no doubt is the real decisive factor in cold war, in that it keeps it cold, or at least prevents it boiling over into world conflagration—one can hardly describe the operations in Korea as cold except in the physical sense in the vile Korean winter. Air forces have essential parts to play in cold war—in support of the land forces, in transport, communication, air supply and so on. And we should not overlook that there are still circumstances in which the air can economically assume the primary rôle, on the method of air control as exercised by the R.A.F. on some wild fringes of the empire between the wars. Nevertheless, the main burden of the cold war falls on the armies. And it is not only in the "Koreas," it is not only in conditions such as those in Malaya and Kenya and Indo-China, that we need the forces to deal with limited threats in a limited way. Even in Europe on the frontiers of freedom there must be a reasonably adequate show of force there on the ground for all to see, not only to sustain the morale of exposed populations but to act, so to speak, as a fire brigade, to counter the tactics of infiltration and oppose a bastion to the technique of the *fait accompli*. Who can say, for instance, that if there were no land and supporting air forces in Germany, there would not be infiltration across the borders of the Federal Republic by the Communist-led People's Police—which already exists in strength complete with tanks and artillery in the Soviet zone—starting no doubt with minor encroachments, feeling the way and leading up on an ever-increasing scale and tempo to serious incursions with which the federal frontier police would be powerless to deal. That sort of thing—like the Communist attempt on Greece, which was finally beaten down by the Greek Regular Army with air support—is unlikely to happen if there are regular troops on the spot and, if it does, can be handled without the extreme sanction of air power.

Finally, if the deterrent were to fail and the Red Army to be set in motion towards the West, our armies and tactical air forces would have the essential rôle of a holding and delaying force, to blunt the enemy offensive and give time for air power to take effect. I believe that can be done without great masses of men. We could do it with far smaller forces than hitherto envisaged, provided they are properly organized, equipped and trained for the job. Five years ago Dr. Vannevar Bush wrote: "It is certain that the fully prepared lines of a competent industrialized nation are not going to be broken by an enemy of equal size unless the latter is capable of operating effectively in the field large masses of highly advanced technical equipment, and this is true even assuming the presence of atomic bombs in moderate quantity on both sides." [3] I believe that today we can say much more than that. It is only prudent to assume that the Russians are capable of using highly advanced technical equipment in the field, and the Red Army is certainly of more than equal size to anything we are likely to oppose to it. Nevertheless, unlike in air and sea-air warfare, I believe that in land-air warfare the scientific development of modern weapons has lent tremendous strength to the defence. It seems to me that the modern land mine, the recoilless anti-tank weapon with the shaped charge, the proximity fuse for artillery and (as recently most effectively demonstrated by the 2nd Allied Tactical Air Force in Germany) the variable-timed airburst fuse for

[3] *Modern Arms and Free Men*, Simon and Schuster, 1949.

bombs, the development of tactical atomic weapons for armies as well as air forces which, as President Eisenhower has told us, have virtually achieved conventional status, even perhaps the use of radio-active by-products to create contaminated belts of ground in special areas—all these surely add up to a far greater accretion of strength to the defence than to the offensive on land. The make and shape of our armies should be adjusted accordingly. Nearly twenty years ago, in a plea for a highly armoured and motorized British Army, I wrote, "If there is one lesson which emerges more clearly than another from the last war in Europe [i.e. 1914-18] it is that a breakthrough is only practicable if it can be carried to its conclusion before the enemy is able to move his reserves to the threatened point. The qualities required of those reserves are, therefore: first, the capacity for rapid movement, which involves as high a degree as possible of immunity from the delaying effect of hostile air action; secondly, the highest possible degree of tactical mobility and flexibility, to enable them to deal with the situation by manoeuvre—by finding flanks instead of merely opposing a fresh defensive front which can be turned or broken again; and thirdly, the maximum striking capacity." [4] If these qualities are important in the attack, they are, if anything, even more so in defence, and my conclusion in 1936 was that the British land contribution to a Continental alliance should take the form of a relatively small but highly mobile armoured strategic reserve for counterattack. Writing with the philosophic detachment of the scientist, Dr. Vannevar Bush casts doubts on the ability of the tank to retain its supremacy in land warfare. As one who saw something at first hand of the

[4] "Gold Medal Essay," *Journal of the Royal United Service Institution*, Vol. LXXXII, No. 527.

German armoured rush across Europe in 1940, I think no one can fail to have been struck by the almost hypnotic effect on Allied morale of the brutal audacity of the enemy armoured columns. But even then there was no reason why they should have had it as much their own way as they did. It is true that we lacked suitable anti-tank weapons in anything approaching adequate numbers, but once the breakthrough got under way there was no real organized attempt to stop it—the German panzers even refuelled at local filling stations, which were seldom destroyed. Perhaps above all the enemy armoured divisions did not have to worry about their flanks, because they knew we lacked the mobile armoured reserve for counterattack.[5]

From these considerations the proper pattern for the land forces of the Atlantic Alliance surely emerges. For those that might have to stem the first rush of invasion in Europe, the core should be highly mobile armoured divisions with powerful self-propelled artillery, covered and supported by the tactical air forces, some of whose functions may in time be more economically assumed by advanced types of weapons on the ground, such as atomic artillery. These first line forces should be supplemented by some infantry divisions for the mobile holding rôle, but mainly by local semi-static forces on a new and relatively inexpensive model, of which another political advantage would be that, while they could be highly effective in defence, they would be totally unsuitable for the strategic offensive rôle. It is to be hoped that we shall not have to wait much longer for the embodiment of the twelve German divisions envisaged in the proposals for a European

[5] It is an amazing fact that the British, having invented the tank in 1916, went to war twenty-three years later without one single armoured division.

Defence Community. As soon as possible after they come into being, the majority of them should be organized and equipped as armoured divisions. But twelve divisions by themselves are not going to assure the defence of Germany against invasion, and they should be supplemented, not by many more on the same model, still less by traditional infantry divisions of the *Landwehr* type, but mainly by a highly trained, semi-static Home Guard armed primarily with anti-tank guns and with light automatics as the personal weapon. The Federal Republic, and ultimately all re-unified Germany, should be covered with a network of these units composed of local men, knowing every inch of the ground, every coppice and stream, lane and side street, responsible for the defence of their own *kreis* and town or village and inspired by the knowledge that they are protecting their own homes and their own kith and kin. They should be responsible for the storage and protection of land mines in peace and for laying the mine fields when so directed, using locally requisitioned civilian transport. They should also, where appropriate, be in charge of strategic demolitions in their zone—the well-known unwillingness of people to touch off demolitions when the time comes is less likely to be present when the alternative is Russian occupation. There is no "Maginot" conception in this, no cowering in deep concrete shelters. The Germans have shown in two world wars a remarkable aptitude for tough, resourceful individual fighting in defence, and are not lightly cowed by armoured or air superiority on the part of their enemy. The personnel would be young and middle-aged men who had received their initial training in the late war or as conscripts in the regular divisions, for which a proportion of them would be available to bring units up to war establishments on mobilization and to find casualty replacements. Units of this type, organized on a territorial basis, would be infinitely less costly than regular formations, since they would need none of the masses of transport, armoured vehicles, elaborate signal communications and administrative "tail" that are essential in a regular army. They would be more like the old *khassadars* of the Indian Frontier. And their job would be to block every road and destroy every tank and armoured carrier moving across country in their zone—and when they could do no more, then pull out or blow up their guns, and cut and run for the next belt of posts in their rear. Against a defence system of this kind, covered by adequate air (including especially "intruders" for destroying soft-skinned petrol-tankers on the roads behind the enemy) and supported by really mobile, hard-hitting regular armoured reserves, I should be surprised if General Guderian would welcome the job of conducting an armoured invasion of his own country, even in great numerical strength. And I do not see how Germany's neighbours could reasonably fear a *Reichswehr* thus organized, whether it were within the E.D.C. or not, since it would be quite incapable of invading them.

The organization suggested above for the German land and air forces should be reproduced, adapted and modified as necessary to meet local conditions, by the other European partners in N.A.T.O., including the Turks on the eastern end of the line. Experience in the Maquis has shown the French to have admirable qualities for this almost guerilla type of fighting required by the new-model Home Guard. The terrain and conditions in Greece as in Italy are suitable for it; the Yugoslavs [6] have shown themselves adept at it; while the tough fighting men of Turkey

[6] I am aware that Yugoslavia is not in N.A.T.O., but in the event of war she would have an important gap to fill in the Allied line.

would seem to lend themselves well to the same sort of thing, and I should not care to be the enemy general assigned to turn the Turkish eastern flank via the Tabriz gap, against this kind of defence supported by air forces with the tactical atomic weapon.

For Great Britain and the United States the position is rather different. As far as Britain is concerned—and it seems to me that similar, though by no means exactly parallel conditions apply in America—we can neither afford nor do we really need to maintain the whole of the Regular Army on the very high standard of armament and equipment essential for those portions of it that may be required for operations in Europe—what might be described as the "first line" army. We should be in a position to reinforce the British Army of the Rhine in a crisis to a very limited extent—two or three divisions at most. The reinforcing divisions must, of course, be on the same scale of equipment and reserves, and if possible they should be regular divisions. But if they were required, they would be wanted very quickly, and we can not assume that we shall always have two or three regular divisions available when the need arises. This difficulty might be surmounted by maintaining a pool of "first line" equipment and reserves in the United Kingdom available for two or three divisions of the first-line strategic reserve. And two or three Territorial divisions should be allotted to that reserve, as an alternative to regular divisions in case the latter are not in hand when required, either to reinforce B.A.O.R. or the Middle East or to take part in one of these possible "other Koreas," for which experience in the real Korea has shown that the highest scale of equipment and reserves may be necessary. Further than this, we can not afford to maintain either the rest of the Regular or of the Territorial Army on first-class war scales. So the "second line"—the balance of the Regular Army after B.A.O.R.—should be armed and equipped to second line, cold war scales, not only of unit arms and equipment but of the war reserves of ammunition, vehicles and so on which in these days are such an appallingly expensive item. Such scales, while not ideal, would be adequate for the sort of overseas commitments for which the British Regular Army is constantly required and which they fulfil so well.

There are, of course, organizational and training difficulties about this proposal, but they are not insuperable; we can not afford to allow the organizational or the training dog to wag the strategic tail in this respect, which is one of those in which the best can so easily become the enemy of the good. It is sometimes suggested that air mobility could justify actual reductions in the strength of our land forces. I doubt whether such a hope has any justification, anyway in present conditions. That air mobility can be of the utmost value has many times been proved— for instance in the move of the 3rd Division and 16th Parachute Brigade to the Middle East three years ago. And the equipment and supporting weapons of the Army should all, as far as possible, be designed to be air transportable. We can save money, and what is more we can save wasting a lot of valuable time, especially for the short-service soldier, by air trooping instead of moving men by sea. But for some time to come I see no prospect of reducing the strength of the Regular Army by virtue of the high strategic mobility involved in air transport.

For the "third line," the Territorial Army—and this of course applies with equal force to the National Guard in the United States—the Home Guard rôle suggested for

Continental armies is clearly not appropriate. But it is surely only realistic to recognize the virtual certainty that, apart from the few Territorial divisions of the first-line strategic reserve, their rôle in the event of another great war will be home defence, which, in effect, will be mainly (though not entirely) what we now know as Civil Defence. That function in any future great war will no longer be appropriate to the physically limited, the ladies and the old gentlemen who so gallantly performed it in the Battle of Britain. In the terrible conditions which must be anticipated, the work of rescue and evacuation, fire-fighting and decontamination, and maintenance of the minimum essential services would be a job for highly organized, specially trained and equipped, mobile units under military discipline. There will also be a limited requirement for a rôle which again will no longer be suitable for the type of middle-aged patriot who so nobly filled the ranks of the Home Guard in 1940, namely the defence of certain especially vital points (which need not be specified) and of certain air bases against low flying air attack or the possibility of an airborne *coup-de-main*. I do not for a moment believe in the bogey of large-scale airborne invasion that is sometimes conjured up. Even in 1941, in the Invasion Committee referred to in an earlier chapter, we did not take that danger seriously and pointed out that, while it might do damage, it would certainly be overwhelmed unless it could be supported almost immediately by seaborne invasion. But there are a limited number of objectives, and the bases of our atomic bombers are high among them, of which the destruction would be so important to an enemy that he might conceivably risk a desperate suicide attempt to destroy them by airborne shock troops. It is not very likely, if only because it would probably be less difficult to do it with atomic bombs, but it can not be entirely ruled out, especially at the very outset of a war.

These important functions are by no manner of means beneath the dignity of the Territorial Army—indeed they might be vital to our survival. And I can be cleared of any accusation of wisdom after the event in saying that I never believed that either the Civil Defence or Home Guard responsibilities could be met by trying to organize them on 1940 lines in present conditions. It is all very well to call upon people with many other things to do to join the Home Guard or a Civil Defence Rescue Squad in war or in times of acute and obvious danger, but I did not believe—and events have borne me out—that to try to organize them in the conditions even of this sort of "peace" would be a success. In any event not only are the personnel available not of a suitable age to meet the more exacting requirements of a possible future war, but they should in war be more than ever fully employed in their normal avocations.

The landing at Inchon in 1950 showed that there may be a need for amphibious operations in small wars, and there is therefore a case for maintaining some small forces specially trained and equipped for this purpose—the traditional rôle of the Marines. But here is a field in which the specialist is rather liable to run away with himself, and we should set our faces against heavy expenditure on special craft and equipment designed for large-scale operations on the lines of the "Overlord" landings, which will never again be practicable in the face of a first-class enemy—the atom bomb is superlatively lethal when burst in water. Rather the same considerations apply to airborne forces. It would probably astonish the reader were I able (which I am not because as far as I know the necessary sums have never been done) to state the cost in manpower and material of the airborne forces of the late war, complete with all the aircraft and manpower devoted to training and carrying them and tugging their gliders, compared with their impact upon the enemy. They could certainly find no place in the early stages of another great war—they are far too vulnerable in conditions of anything but virtually complete air supremacy. Nevertheless, experience in Indo-China has shown that they can be valuable in small wars and again there is a case for retaining a few units of this type, though this is a direction in which appreciable economies might well be found, perhaps more in the United States than in Britain.

Finally, there will be some, no doubt, who hope that a New Look in defence will do away with the need for national service.[7] I think it more than doubtful whether we shall be able in the foreseeable future to man the land and air forces that must be retained even on a reduced scale, entirely by voluntary enlistment. I am indeed far from sure that it is desirable on social grounds to abolish national service; it has its economic and industrial disadvantages and there are certain difficulties about combining the compulsory with the voluntary principle. But not the least of the causes of some of our present domestic discontents is the lack of discipline in so many homes and schools, and of the sense of social service among too many of our people. Whether the boy is destined in later life to be a bishop or a bartender, a farmer or a salesman, I think he will be a better *man*—and probably a better bishop or bartender, farmer or salesman—for having had a couple of youthful years of that sort of discipline which leads to self-discipline and self-respect, of hard physical training and of doing a

[7] The draft in the United States.

job for the good of the community instead of merely his own. The regular service has a heavy responsibility to ensure that the young men entrusted to their care for these two formative years do in fact get the right sort of training, social as well as military, and to make the best use of them while they are in the service. I believe on the whole they meet that responsibility well and that the youngster who says his national service was a waste of time is usually—not invariably but usually—the sort who considers anything a waste of time but looking after himself, getting as much money for as little work as he can, being waited on hand and foot by "Mum" and going to the pictures twice a week. And probably even that sort of chap—and they are a small minority—would be an even less desirable member of the community but for his military service.

III

No Englishman with a grain of sense underrates the importance of the naval service, certainly not myself whose experience in the Battle of the Atlantic enhanced my understanding of the maritime affair and my affectionate regard for the Royal Navy. The North Atlantic Treaty Organization, as its very name implies, is a great coalition bound together by sea communications, and as long as there is any possibility of another great war—and, however unlikely, no one can yet say such a thing is impossible—the navies will be needed for the protection of those communications against the deadly menace of the mine and the submarine. Unless we can maintain the essential imports into Britain and Europe, the British people starve and the war effort of N.A.T.O. would wither and perish—the air forces can not fly nor the armies fight without the raw material to make their equipment and the fuel to keep them moving. In the late war the lowest annual rate of imports into the United Kingdom (in 1942) was about thirty-nine million short tons, of which about twelve million were food and twelve million fuel oil and aviation petrol. The monthly rate of indispensable imports in another great war, even if it lasted any length of time (which I can not imagine in an atomic age), could hardly be more and might well be less than in 1942. An imaginative programme of improving the agricultural productivity of our own land (which is anyway overdue) a farseeing stockpile policy and (perhaps very important) the development of nuclear energy for industrial and motive purposes could lead to an important reduction in the import tonnage of food and fuel oil required in war. In addition, I think we can assume that before very long it will be possible to transfer a substantial proportion of essential imports from the sea to the air in emergency. It was not the battle fleet that was the real backbone of British sea power in our palmy days, nor the greyhounds of the Atlantic; it was the freighters, the tramp steamers and tankers, cargo ships of all types and sizes all over the world—the "dirty British coaster with the salt-caked smoke stack" of Masefield's poem. The same thing will probably be true of air power. We have hardly touched the fringe of the possibilities of cargo carriage by air. There is a great future for the specially designed freighter aircraft with engines, such as the compound type, having very economical fuel consumption, capable of carrying heavy loads over great distances at moderate speeds, and operating from small airfields at varying heights above sea level. Five years ago an Anglo-American transport fleet of about four hundred aircraft, many of them uneconomical, obsolete types including converted bombers, were lifting cargo, including some petrol, over the short hop into only three airfields round beleaguered Berlin, at a peak rate of over a quarter-million short tons a month—three million a year. It is surely not unduly optimistic to suggest that in twenty-five years from now it would be perfectly possible in war to fly essential imports into the United Kingdom, over the necessarily longer distances, at three times the peak rate of the Berlin airlift. The result of these developments will not be to make Britain independent of seaborne imports in war—far from it. That is highly improbable in the foreseeable future. But it will make our problem very much easier in that, instead of it being literally vital to continue, week in week out in all weathers throughout the year, to bring great convoys on a regular cycle through submarine-infested waters into British ports, the numbers of convoys could be substantially reduced, thus correspondingly easing the load on the escort fleet and enabling it to provide far stronger escorts for each convoy. It will also mean that when necessary it will not be fatal to suspend the sailing of convoys altogether for a period, while a specially formidable concentration of enemy submarines is dealt with.

However, these things be some way off, and as far ahead as we need look today the ability of Britain to survive and of the forces of N.A.T.O. this side of the Atlantic to fight in war will depend on the capacity of the navies and air forces to prevent our shipping being sunk at an intolerable rate. It is the navies' misfortune that aircraft today have lost much of their efficacy against the submarine. In 1943, the peak year of the Battle of the Atlantic which saw the decisive defeat of the U-boat attack on our shipping, aircraft were the decisive arm and sank twice as many U-boats in the Atlantic as did ships. With the advent of the schnorkel and high-speed submerged the modern submarine becomes a real submarine instead of merely a submersible, and has far less to fear from aircraft. It is difficult to envisage this balance being redressed in the near future, though fortunately with the new weapons we could look forward to substantially better results from attack on the submarine menace at its source than in the late war.[8] Aircraft would still be valuable partners of the surface ship in the anti-submarine rôle, but there is no getting away from the fact that, in the absence of some at present unforeseen scientific development, the main burden would fall upon the surface ship, and perhaps the submarine in the "fighter" rôle.

Nevertheless if further economies must be found in defence expenditure, it is impossible to resist the conclusion that they must and can be found in the sea service, and one's thoughts must inevitably turn to those components of the fleets which are least relevant to the main threats with which our sea communications would be faced—the submarine and the mine. It is easy to understand the romantic spell which binds to the imagination of our people the great grey ships which, with their great grey guns, were for so long the mainstay and symbol of sea power. Now that the great grey gun has given way to the little grey aeroplane, the aircraft carrier has usurped the place of the battleship. But in these days we can not afford any luxuries, not even the luxury of sentiment, and the great ship has to justify itself beyond all reasonable argument before its retention can be afforded priority over other components of defence. We merely confuse the issue by *ex cathedra*

---

[8] Even then it accounted for more U-boats in commission than did the aircraft carriers—sixty-six against fifty-three, not including the many U-boats destroyed by bombing before completion. (Note: a kill shared with some other anti-submarine agency is counted as a half.)

pronouncements like "it is important that at all times a carrier striking force, well equipped and fully worked up, should be available" to the British Home Fleet.[9] Why? What would that striking force be required *for* in war? What is it going to strike? These great ships with their escorting cruisers and destroyer screens, and with all their aircraft and associated shore establishments, are appallingly expensive to build and maintain, and this is a field in which a balanced appreciation of the economics of defence—Dr. Vannevar Bush's missile [10]—is specially important. We must ask ourselves *first* whether the impact of the aircraft carrier upon our only imaginable enemies in a future great war is likely to justify the cost involved—whether its action in an improbable war is likely to hurt them more than its cost will certainly damage us, war or no war; and whether there is any vital interest of our own that can only be secured, or secured less expensively than by other means, by the aircraft carrier. For this we must rely in the main, though not entirely, on the experience of the only war, of the same sort as that we have now to consider, in which carriers have ever been engaged. We are not preparing to fight another war like that against Japan in which the relentless advance of air power across the Pacific would have been impossible without carrier-based support; we should therefore consider the war against the Germans and Italians in the Atlantic and European waters, including the Mediterranean. Secondly, we must satisfy ourselves that the carrier has a reasonable chance of remaining afloat in the face of modern methods of attack.

In those theatres of the late war which we are here considering, the Royal Navy had in commission at various

[9] *The Times*, 5 January 1954.
[10] See p. 51.

times on or after the outbreak of war a total of fifty-eight
aircraft carriers of various types, which were supplemented
in the Atlantic by seven U.S. light carriers.[11] Under our *first*
heading, no one suggests that the carrier has a great future
as a counter to the enemy mine menace. Against our next
most formidable enemy, the submarine, carriers played an
active part last time. A curious impression has, however,
gained ground since the war that the most deadly enemy
of the U-boat was a unit known by the romantic title of
Hunter-killer group, comprising a light carrier and a number of surface anti-submarine craft. Even Dr. Bush goes so
far as to suggest that it was these units carrying the war to
the enemy that turned the tide against the U-boat.[12] Unfortunately this impression is not borne out by the facts.
It is well-known that the "customer is always right" and
the fact that the most deadly enemy of the U-boat was the
radar-fitted shore-based aircraft of Coastal Command is confirmed by Admiral Doenitz himself. Actually only fourteen
U-boats were killed in the Atlantic by a combination of
surface ships and carrier-borne aircraft (there were another
five in the Pacific); the back of the U-boat menace to our
Atlantic convoys had been broken by the beginning of
August 1943, and up to that date carrier-borne aircraft had
only been involved in a total of sixteen kills since the outbreak of war, of which three only were in combination
with surface ships. The totals of German and Italian
U-boats sunk at sea in the Atlantic and Mediterranean
theatres were fourteen by Hunter-killer units, forty by submarines, forty-six [13] by carrier-borne aircraft, 271 [14] by shore-

[11] There may have been one or two more, but if so they killed no
U-boats. On the other hand, a few British carriers were stationed in
the Indian Ocean and Far Eastern waters.

[12] *Modern Arms and Free Men*, Simon and Schuster, 1949.

[13] Includes one by an air-laid mine.

[14] Both these figures include sixteen by mines.

based aircraft, 299 [14] by surface ships and thirty-seven shared by shore-based aircraft and surface ships in combination. It is difficult to claim that the percentage (just over 7 per cent) of U-boats falling to the carriers is sufficiently impressive to carry the conviction that they are an indispensable adjunct to any anti-submarine campaign of the future, particularly in view of the serious falling off since the late war in the efficacy of any type of aircraft against submarines, which has already been noted. It is true that they were able to kill some U-boats beyond the range of shore-based aircraft, but that is a difficulty which could usually be avoided in future by the selective routing of convoys.

Another factor in the economics of maritime warfare is the value of any particular weapon against enemy surface ships. In this respect the record of the U.S. carriers in the Pacific is, no doubt, impressive. But in the war we are now considering, again it can not be claimed that the British and American carriers paid a dividend commensurate with the resources invested in them. Aircraft operating from these carriers destroyed twenty-five enemy warships and fifty-two merchant ships, as compared with 612 and 846 respectively for shore-based aircraft. Anyway, in another war we should not be particularly interested in destroying the enemy's shipping, which could not seriously affect his war effort. We have, however, to reckon with the possibility of some cruisers of a formidable type breaking out into the Atlantic, and they might be a serious menace to our convoys. This is a factor to be taken into account in weighing the case for aircraft carriers in the N.A.T.O. navies.[15]

---

[15] It is incidentally of some interest to note that the Soviets have not gone in for carriers.

Air attack on our Atlantic convoys was not the deadly menace that might have been expected. It did assume serious proportions after the fall of Norway and we lost ninety-five ships (out of a total of 650 sunk) to German aircraft by the end of 1940. Most of these attacks were beyond the cover of our short-range shore-based fighters, and against them fighters catapulted off merchant ships, and later flying from a light carrier, were invaluable. By the end of 1941 the menace receded, largely no doubt owing to the action of the ship-borne fighters, and little more was heard of it in later years. Ship-borne aircraft destroyed a total of something like fifty aircraft during the war in Atlantic and Northwest European waters. It would be very unsafe to assume that this form of attack on shipping would not be far more serious in another war. The anti-aircraft protection of convoys far out at sea can not be undertaken by shore-based fighters, and here again is a *prima facie* case for the retention of some carriers.

Another function performed on several occasions by the carriers was fighter cover of opposed landings, as at Salerno. I have already stated my view that amphibious operations against a first-class enemy are a thing of the past, so we need not include that function in the balance sheet. Some importance, however, is attached in N.A.T.O. planning to air cover and support by carrier task forces for land operations on the flanks—no doubt that would be a function of the U.S. Sixth Fleet in the Mediterranean. The permanent value of carrier task forces for this purpose is partly dependent upon the question of the vulnerability of big ships, which is considered later. But apart from that, here again is Dr. Bush's missile. Is this the most efficient and most economical way of providing air support for operations on land? It has some advantages; for instance it is argued that it raises fewer political difficulties to base air-craft in a ship than on a land base in someone else's coun-try, though it must be admitted that this factor does not seem to have weighed very heavily with the United States in the Mediterranean area. But when out of the wrappings of huge heavily armed ships, escorting cruisers and destroy-ers, oilers and supply ships, anti-submarine aircraft and fighters to protect the task force from attack, there ulti-mately emerges the somewhat modest jewel of the striking force actually available for the support of the land cam-paign—a force whose operations can in the nature of things only be somewhat intermittent—the defence economist is bound to regard it as a rather doubtful dividend. It is true that the cost of shore bases is high these days, but it pales into insignificance compared with that of the Sixth Fleet.

Lastly there is the use of the carrier as a mobile advanced base for participation in the strategic air offensive, for which the United States are building and proposing to build a number of vast ships at a cost which soars into the financial stratosphere. Says Dr. Bush of this, "The primary mission of our Navy in war is to interrupt enemy sea com-merce and to make it possible for our commerce to move safely to supply our allies and our fighting forces over-seas. . . . Certainly until we have the means fully in hand for discharging the primary mission it would be foolhardy to seek out new tasks for great ships, such as participation in strategic bombing, merely for the sake of having great ships. Their cost is large and their impregnability ques-tionable. On the other hand if there is an essential aspect of strategic bombing that can be effected only from car-riers and if they can be defended with reasonable effort and assurance, by all means build them before it is too

late." [16] At this point our consideration must spill over into
the second factor mentioned on page 99 above—the vulnerability of ships—if only because of its relevance to the
economic factor. A great ship of this sort, if in fact it is
considered effective for the purpose for which it is designed,
ipso facto becomes an enormously important objective,
worth great sacrifice on the part of an enemy to destroy.
One must assume that it has been made impervious to the
torpedo, though how it can achieve the same immunity
against the modern mine, I do not know. I think it will be
very difficult indeed, if not quite impossible, to make it
indestructible by a weapon of which a crude prototype sank
the Italian battleship *Roma* ten years ago, the guided bomb
—next time with an atomic warhead. The guided bomb of
the near future will be launchable from a range beyond that
at which fighters will be able to intercept on receipt of
radar early warning in the ship, which will be "a clear
target to radar and a clear target to the guided bomb." [17]
It is the guided bomb which I think is the crucial factor
in this whole problem of the carrier for whatever purpose.
It is not inconceivable that a means of defence may be
found against it, which will no doubt have to include a
screen of early warning aircraft and/or surface vessels. The
practical difficulties of future anti-aircraft defence in bulk
which, in an earlier chapter, I have suggested rules out the
practicability of overall defence of whole countries, are not
so prohibitive for a few great ships. Whether it would be
practicable for convoys and their escorting carriers is another question. Only one thing seems certain about it, if it
is found, namely that it will add enormously to the already
astronomical cost of the Forrestal-class carrier. As to the

[16] *Modern Arms and Free Men*, Simon and Schuster, 1949.
[17] *Ibid.*

strategic value of these mobile atomic-bomber bases, I do not deny that it would be nice to have them; they would add still further to the Soviet's already acute problem of all-round defence of that vast area. But I do not believe they are an essential part of the Deterrent, or that the lack of them would make a decisive difference to the strategic air offensive if the Deterrent fails. Let me sum it up again in Dr. Bush's words: "The mission of the Navy will be as important, and as difficult, as it has ever been in history. It will need to employ modern techniques to the utmost and in ample quantity," and he goes on to say, "The Navy has plenty to do to combat the submarine and protect shipping against enemy aircraft, and for this it needs ample strength." [18] To that it is necessary to add the mine. It is no secret that the navies of N.A.T.O. have not yet got ample strength to deal with these deadly threats—far from it. And I think it untenable to support things like these floating bomber-bases, or striking forces for the British Home Fleet, as long as we are so deficient in the arms that might be vital to our survival in another war. For some time to come I think there will be a case for N.A.T.O. maintaining some carriers for anti-aircraft escort of convoys, and perhaps a few more to provide against the threat by enemy cruisers. Experience has shown that there is also a use for them in cold war, when our interests are threatened by disorder in inaccessible places. They are, in fact, the modern equivalent of the Victorian cruiser. Their days are, no doubt, numbered and the time will come when there will be a better way of doing the job [19] than packing a lot of ordinary aircraft into one steel hull that would

[18] *Ibid.*
[19] High-speed fighters capable of vertical take-off and landing are an important example.

obviously be the first target for attack. Meanwhile I believe the navies of N.A.T.O. have a good many more of these great ships than can be justified. To quote Dr. Bush again, "We need a Navy intent on the full accomplishment of its main mission and not diverted by the sirens of more spectacular fields." [20] I do not think the full saving that would be justified can all be counted as gain; some should go to increasing our defence against the mine and the submarine. Nevertheless there should still be substantial economies.

I have drawn fully in this section on the writings of a great American defence scientist, who can reasonably be expected to take a dispassionate view, in the hope that it may emphasize the need to examine these problems objectively and not in any spirit of inter-service rivalry. Service traditions and loyalties are excellent things, and indeed essential to fighting efficiency, but they should not be allowed to distort our judgment. After all, the overriding interest of all of us is to ensure that our children and grandchildren do not have to endure the dreary horrors of another world war, and incidentally we would none of us mind keeping a bit more of our own money instead of handing so much of it over to the tax collectors. I confess myself as being in one respect in disagreement with the man whom I regard as the greatest of all air force officers, Lord Trenchard, in that I think that as long as there are aircraft carriers, their aircraft and crews had better be part of the navy. It may not be logical, but I believe it is practical—the other way [21] just would not work, human nature being what it is. Men who live in ships and operate off ships are in practice more conveniently part of the navy,

[20] *Op. cit.*
[21] A system under which the carriers belong to the navy and the aircraft and crews to the R.A.F.

though there is no kind of black art about air action over the sea. For the navy's part I think they would be much better off if they did not have so many shore establishments. To me the sailor in his bell-bottomed trousers looks as out of place in the green fields of Somerset as he does on the plains of Kansas. There is no earthly reason why the R.A.F. should not do the shore work for the Fleet Air Arm, and a return to that basis—which underlay the Inskip award of 1937 [22] when the control of naval aviation was passed to the Admiralty—would effect another economy in defence overheads.

IV

It is not as inconsequent as it may seem to go on to say, with the utmost emphasis, that one of the best known ways of wasting public money is the overlapping and duplication of overheads that inevitably results from having four or five different air forces. The only possible exception to the golden rule that there should be one air force and one only, charged with carrying out air operations over the land and over the sea, is where experience has conclusively proved that as a practical matter of organization and procedure it literally will not work. Another exception might be if war experience had proved that in any specific function or field the principle of the unity of air power is not operationally efficient. The R.A.F. in the late war provided no such example—it did not have an opportunity of proving that it could operate carrier-borne aircraft as efficiently as it did the Coastal Command. In the United States there are, in effect, four air forces—the U.S.A.F. proper, Navy, Army and Marine Corps Aviation—five if the Coast Guard is included. There is little wonder that the defence appro-

[22] Decided primarily on the advice of Sir Winston Churchill (*The Gathering Storm*, Houghton Mifflin, 1948, Appendix B).

priations are on such an astronomical scale. It is not only the antithesis of economy but a denial of the first principles of sound, strategic application of air power—flexibility and concentration of force at the decisive point. We are more fortunate in Britain. And it is devoutly to be hoped that no future British government will forget how sensible and farseeing were their predecessors in initiating and maintaining the principle of a single, autonomous Royal Air Force, with the one exception of the transfer to the Admiralty of the Fleet Air Arm in 1937 which, as I have earlier implied, was an exceedingly expensive experiment.

It would be idle to deny that sectional pressure to abolish Coastal Command by transferring to the Royal Navy the responsibility for what have come to be known as maritime air operations from shore bases does still occasionally make itself felt. The story of the Battle of the Atlantic is a decisive demolition of the argument that the R.A.F. was an unworthy partner of the Royal Navy in the war at sea. And to disunite the Royal Air Force at a time when the defeat of another submarine attack on our shipping is bound to rest more on destroying U-boats at source than sinking them at sea, would indeed be the climax of absurdity.

The air is indivisible and the only principle that makes sense is that the man who fights in the air should be an airman, the man who fights at sea a sailor, and the man who fights on land a soldier.[23] And, I repeat, the only exception to that rule should be where its application is organizationally impractical or operationally inefficient.

[23] With great respect to that fine corps, the R.A.F. regiment to whom the rest of the service owes so much, I have always regarded its existence as a regrettable necessity, and it always struck me as wrong in principle (though it worked out all right in practice) that I should have had a large fleet of small seagoing vessels manned by men in R.A.F. blue in the Air-Sea Rescue units of Coastal Command.

The Primary Arm

Allied air power was decisive in the war in Western Europe. Hindsight inevitably suggests that it might have been employed differently or better in some respects. Nevertheless it was decisive.

Summary Report [European War],
United States Strategic Bombing Survey.

I

It should be clear from the previous chapter that I am not one of those, if there be any such (and I have never met one), who think that air power by itself can defeat a first-class enemy. It did not do so last time, though I think if we had been able to wield it with fewer inevitable diversions to other tasks and without certain political handicaps of which the effect might have been foreseen, it would have ended the war earlier and saved a vast amount of human suffering and loss. It was always clear after 1940 that land forces would have to return to the continent of Europe. But air power properly used might have enabled them to return as an occupying and rehabilitating agency on a march table, instead of on the operation order that hurled them against the Normandy beaches. "Nevertheless it was decisive," and the words at the head of this chapter were written not by unbalanced "air enthusiasts" but by the D'Olier Committee, a body of analytically minded civilians and military men with special experience and training, who were able to survey the record objectively and draw their own conclusions. Since 1945 the astonishing development of nuclear and thermo-nuclear energy and of high-speed jet-propelled bombers has transformed the whole dimension and nature of the problem. They have brought the Great Deterrent into world affairs and, if that should fail of its purpose, would be far more rapidly decisive in another great war. There can be no certainty about the nature of a future war, except perhaps that it would be quite different from the last and probably from most people's conception of another. But with weapons of mass destruction on either side I can not conceive it lasting anything like as long as the wars we have known. Airmen are popularly supposed to be fervent disciples of the late General Giulio Douhet. I confess I have never read his works, but understand that he made the mistake of being a bit too far ahead of his time—1939-45 proved him wrong; another war in our time might well prove him right.

The earlier chapters of this book have developed the theme that modern air power armed with the weapon of mass destruction has had the effect that total war has abolished itself, and hence that it is above all in the interest of the peace of the world to retain what I have called the Great Deterrent as a first charge on our resources. It has been suggested that it may very well be scientifically possible to devise defensive weapons that would neutralize the bomber as we now know it, and conceivably to do the same for its successor, the unmanned bomber or long-range controlled missile, but that anything in the nature of an over-all air defence of great countries would be beyond the capacity of their economic or human resources—in other words that, while perhaps scientifically feasible, it is not a practical economic proposition. The validity of this claim is decisive to the whole issue and deserves a critical glance, since if it is not tenable then the Deterrent itself is not valid, depending as it does on the presumption that, if in fact the issue were put to the test, the atomic (and in the near future the hydrogen) bomb would have the strategic result implied.

The eminent scientific authority from whom I have quoted so freely in the last chapter, writing about five years ago, expressed the view that "conventional mass bombing may be obsolete." [1] That was a cautious understatement; I do not think there is any doubt that it is already obsolete. The cost of modern long-range bombers is so immense that no one would consider arming them with T.N.T. or incendiaries. Those weapons were utterly catastrophic in Japan and Germany, but we can no longer think in terms of thousand-bomber raids going on month after month as we knew them last time. The modern bomber must, and of course can, pack a punch which is immeasurably greater, say of the order of five thousand times as great as the conventional bomb loads of the 1939-45 war, and, of course, even that will be multiplied enormously in the thermo-nuclear weapon. There is no question of the lone bomber carrying the atomic weapon, which Dr. Bush quite rightly says would probably get shot down; so the defences would be confused by sending in relatively large formations some of which might carry conventional weapons while others would be equipped with the appropriate "counter measure" gear to deal with the

[1] Dr. Vannevar Bush, *Modern Arms and Free Men*, Simon and Schuster, 1949.

enemy defences—the modern equivalent of the long-range fighter escorts of ten years ago. Modern methods of control and reporting, modern computers and the proximity fuse in A.A. artillery have put an end to great fleets of relatively slow bombers operating at the moderate altitudes of the last war, even against existing armament in fighters; indeed the moderate altitudes are the last at which to fly— really low altitude attack, as Dr. Bush has pointed out, can be very formidable, in spite of the navigational difficulties, which can be surmounted. We have not got to wait for the deadly long-range ground-to-air guided missile, which is further away than we are sometimes led to believe, to put an end to anything resembling the bombing of the late war. The small air-to-air guided rocket will increase the lethality of the fighter by a decisive factor against anything resembling 1944-45 bombing; it is hardly too much to say that it will turn the effective interception into an almost certain kill, and be the equivalent of an important multiplication of the numerical strength of existing fighter forces.

Dr. Bush suggests that even the high-flying bomber may have only a temporary lease of life. There again he is almost certainly right, but I think it will remain effective long enough to be a decisive factor in our present strategy for the West. At these great altitudes, the margin between maximum and stalling speeds and the radii of turning circles are such as very severely to restrict manoeuvrability and make effective interception of bombers flying at speeds in the neighbourhood of that of sound very difficult.[2] It must be remembered that visual bombing from these

[2] Rather unexpectedly it has not made the dogfight impossible, as Dr. Bush thought, when fighters deliberately choose to engage each other in clear weather, even at heights of about 40,000 feet, as Korea has shown.

heights is not very relevant and attacks will be timed to come in during dark hours and when possible in thick weather. No one expects that an air offensive will achieve what no operation of war that I know of has ever achieved, and get away with it without casualties—very far from it. But, as already pointed out, not even a high rate of attrition will afford adequate protection quickly enough against the weapon of mass destruction. And it will not again be a question of taking for months and years on end the murderous rate of casualties, of which the endurance by the bomber crews of the R.A.F. and U.S.A.F. last time was one of the miracles in the history of war. Dr. Bush has pointed out that radar bomb-sights can be jammed, while thick weather or artificial smoke screens may thwart other means of homing guided bombs onto their targets. It is quite possible that the uncannily accurate precision bombing that we knew in the later stages of the last war will never be repeated. But we have now to consider the weapons of 1954 and after. It is a measure of the amazing advance in the development of these new weapons in recent years that so far-seeing and well-informed an authority as Dr. Bush, writing in 1949, could talk in terms of "placing a few bombs, even atomic bombs, on a few cities" [3] or say with such assurance that "the atomic bomb can not be subdivided. . . . there will be no shells from guns carrying atomic explosives." [4] We now know from President Eisenhower himself that it is far from being a question of a *few* bombs and that the Army, Navy, Air Force and Marine Corps of the United States are all capable of using the atomic weapon. There are already batteries of atomic artillery in General Gruenther's order of battle.

[3] *Modern Arms and Free Men*, Simon and Schuster, 1949.
[4] *Ibid.*

There is a tendency to misread the lessons of the late war in so far as they relate to the bombing of cities and to claim that what is rather contemptuously referred to as "area bombing" can never be decisive. I believe nothing could possibly be further from the truth. Before 1939 we alarmed ourselves unduly by visions of the "knock-out blow," which we now know from experience was a false alarm with the aircraft and the weapons of that day. World War II was the first air war, and no one had any experience of war in the air between first-class powers. Today we have the experience we then lacked. We have seen a country knocked out primarily by air action, and with conventional weapons at that; we have seen the effects of the atomic bomb on the cities of Japan, and know something of the dreadful power of thermo-nuclear explosion. I have the perhaps somewhat unenviable advantage of an experience, which fortunately has been denied to most people, of being in a city which was literally wiped out, with most of its inhabitants, in fifty-five seconds by the great earthquake in Baluchistan in 1935, a far more effective blitz than anything laid on by either side in the late war, except Hiroshima and Nagasaki. When people talk light-heartedly about that sort of thing on a widespread scale not being decisive, I have to tell them with respect that they do not know what they are talking about. No country could survive a month of Quetta earthquakes on all its main centres of population and remain capable of organized resistance. Of the attack on Hamburg in July 1943 the *U.S. Strategic Bombing Survey* says: "No subsequent city raid shook Germany as did that on Hamburg. Documents show that German officials were thoroughly alarmed and there is some indication from interrogation of high officials that Hitler himself thought that further attacks of similar weight might force Germany out of the war." [5] If Hitler thought that, I believe he was right. Unfortunately it was not practicable in the conditions of 1943, to reproduce Hamburg sufficiently often and soon in other similar cities to have a decisive effect; if it could have been done, I believe it would have enforced Germany's surrender. The picture we have to envisage today is not an isolated Hamburg, not a gradually mounting series of blitzes spread over five years, but scores of Hamburgs in the opening month—and then some.

One day, however, the manned bomber as we know it today will be obsolete and its place will be taken by the long-range guided missile, which again will not be a weapon of precision but which will no doubt be capable of hitting cities, even at inter-continental ranges. The Nemesis of the manned bomber seems likely to be the long-range ground-to-air guided missile, not the relatively short-range weapon suitable only for point defence, which is only a bigger and better anti-aircraft gun and would be prohibitively expensive in manpower and material to provide on the necessary scale. It is true that the relatively long-range pilotless interceptor would also be expensive and could not in practice be provided in sufficient numbers to afford over-all protection of really large areas, but there might be enough to make the operations of manned bombers, even at supersonic speeds, prohibitively costly in casualties. It is a difficult equation to assess but we must at any rate assume that the life of the manned bomber will not be indefinitely prolonged—it might even be brought to an end by very highly supersonic manned fighters. Even the pilotless interceptor will be easier to design and produce than the pilot-

[5] Quoted by J. M. Spaight, *Air Power Can Disarm*, Pitman, 1948, p. 75.

less bomber, and it is for that reason decisively important that we should give the highest priority in design and research to the latter. It would be very dangerous, unless the world political climate is very different to what it is today, to have a gap in which the manned bomber is neutralized and the long-range missile not yet available. That is the sort of thing that in these days decides evil men to go to war, not the traditional factors like whether or not the harvest is in. It would be that, and I think that alone, that could invalidate the presumption on which this argument is based.

II

If this argument is accepted, the case for the bomber force as the primary arm of the Free World is unassailable. Indeed what else could we put in its place? Neither armies nor navies can themselves be an effective deterrent though, as I have tried to show, they are part of the Deterrent. Even under the threat of atomic air power, aggression must not be made otherwise too easy. We should not put the temptation to a quick success before the eyes of ambitious men who may have delusions about their ability to survive atomic air action. And, if it came to war, what other means should we have of defeating the Communist coalition— not of winning the war because no one could do that, but of preventing them from extending their domination over the ruins of the Free World, forcing them to withdraw behind their frontiers and freeing the satellite countries from their yoke? Arthur Bryant, the great historian and an impartial judge whose instinct and interest are, indeed, deeply involved in the traditional glories of the British Army and the Royal Navy, has put it mildly by saying that, in another great war against an enemy occupying the bulk of the vast Eurasian land mass, the Allies would have a far tougher nut to crack than they have ever experienced.[6] They would indeed! I imagine no one would be foolish enough to contemplate trying for a decision by land invasion of Russia. And our enemies would be quite impervious to blockade, to our traditional weapon of economic pressure exerted by sea power. Add to which, in the (to me) almost inconceivable event of another war being prolonged for any length of time, it would be the bomber force alone that could create again, as it did last time, that condition of general air mastery that alone can make possible a favourable decision in land or sea campaigns and protect England from devastation.

This is not a plea for a bomber force far greater than anything now envisaged, nor vastly superior in strength to anything that a potential enemy may ever have at his disposal. The strength of an opponent's air force is only a very partial measure of what we need ourselves—even "parity" is a somewhat meaningless yardstick, as we found in Britain in days gone by. We must have a bomber force capable of doing the job. That, of course, involves a certain minimum strength; but the days are past when the number of bombs available was a severely limiting factor. The crux now is to retain our ability to put those bombs down where we want to, if and when we have to, and we should give highest priority to the scientific techniques of navigation and bomb-aiming and to the various methods of defending bombers against modern forms of attack. The force must have its protected bases, must be highly mobile and capable of deployment at the shortest notice, complete with its essential auxiliaries such as transport aircraft and air refuelling units. And, as always in air warfare, it will be

[6] *Illustrated London News*, 17 January 1953.

quality that counts—the technical excellence of the aircraft and the courage, training and battle-readiness of the personnel. If we have that, we need not worry unduly about what the other fellow has; we shall know that we have in hand an instrument that can do what is required of it, and we need no more. We have already in the U.S. Strategic Air Command a superlatively trained striking force that meets many of these desiderata, and that will soon be joined by the V-class bombers of the R.A.F. whose quality will be no less.

It seems appropriate here to refer to a school of thought which has some supporters in England (fortunately neither many nor influential) and which I have heard hinted at in the United States. The idea, which has certain superficial attractions especially when we meditate upon our income-tax returns, is that we British can safely leave the bomber strength of the Free World to the American Air Force. The argument is that our economic capacity is limited; we must have fighters to protect these islands, tactical squadrons to support the Army and transports to give them mobility, and maritime aircraft to co-operate with the Navy. But we really can not afford these very expensive bombers, and anyway why should we? America is rich, she already has an excellent bomber force, so why not leave it to her?

I suppose no British officer knows the United States Air Force better or admires it more than I do. But I believe that to succumb to this idea would be absolutely fatal on two grounds. First, it would obviously be folly for us to compete with the United States in numbers, and no one contemplates any such thing. But the R.A.F. and the British aircraft industry are an invaluable mine of ingenuity and skill, of battle experience, training and aptitude, of invention, design and technique in this bomber trade. The V-class bombers shortly coming into the service are at least as good as any of their kind in the world and our crews have proved in war, and in friendly competition with their American counterparts since the war, to be second to none. I have never found an American Air Force officer who did not feel with me that it would be an evil day for the Alliance if the British were to allow Bomber Command to wither and die. Secondly, and this is even more important, *the bomber is the primary agent of air mastery.* The R.A.F. without Bomber Command would be like Nelson's fleet without its line of battle. We can not live on our historical tradition or on the credit of our past achievements. If we were to leave to any ally, however staunch and loyal, the monopoly of an instrument of such decisive importance in the stupendous issues of war and peace, we should sooner than later sink to the level of a fourth-rate power. In peace we should lose our great influence in Allied policy and planning; in war we should have little influence on the direction of Allied strategy or on the determination of terms of peace. Nor is this merely a military matter; it has a psychological basis. A wise commentator [7] has warned us of "the psychology of defeatism that such a policy might engender. Britain has grown great because Britons in the past have made a habit of standing on their own feet. If we lost that temper, how much else might we not lose with it." To that I would add that this modern battle fleet—this great force of immensely complicated and expensive aircraft—imperatively requires personnel of the very best quality to man it. This thing is so much a matter of life and death to all of us, that no British family of the

[7] "Scrutator" in *The Sunday Times.*

requisite quality should rest content until they have at least one son serving his country in the air.

The United States and Britain are the only partners in the Alliance who have the resources to enable them to maintain a bomber force. But other people have proved in war that they have the right aptitude for this branch of air warfare—the Canadians especially had a well-deserved reputation in Bomber Command and No. 6 Group R.C.A.F. played a noble part in the defeat of Germany. Frenchmen and Dutchmen, Poles and Czechs also manned squadrons of high quality within the framework of the R.A.F. It would be manifestly uneconomical, indeed impossible, for these smaller nations each to attempt to reproduce a sort of microcosm of Bomber Command or the Strategic Air Command. Is it, however, too much to hope that before long we may see squadrons in one or both of these commands manned by Canadians, Frenchmen and men from the Netherlands? It has been suggested that there should eventually be a single N.A.T.O. strategic air force under one supreme command like Saclant or Saceur. That might be logical but I think it unnecessary and on the whole undesirable: unnecessary because the bombers of the R.A.F. and U.S.A.F. have amply demonstrated in three years of war that they can work together on a co-ordinated plan in perfect rhythm and pattern, without being under one over-all commander; undesirable because the relative size of the two components would almost inevitably lead to the supreme commander being an American, and I do not think it healthy for anyone concerned (including the United States) that one partner should hold too many of the high command appointments within the Alliance.

III

Air power obviously comprises more than striking power alone. Indeed too often the term suggests to too many memories the words of the Prime Minister's great tribute to the few of the Battle of Britain, and the impression is very common—perhaps inevitably so because one always understands best the thing that he can see—that air defence is the exclusive province of the fighter. Nothing could be further from the truth. But the fighter is an element in air power second only to the bomber. Before the late war we made the mistake in our planning of underrating the importance of the fighter, and only put that right just in time to provide the force that was primarily instrumental in winning the Battle of Britain—and then perhaps only because of the crowning mercy of the "phony war" period. Even the relatively archaic bombers of that day made a valuable contribution to that battle, and still more to the prevention of invasion across the Channel—more than we realized at the time. An adequate fighter force is, however, a vital element in air defence—it is the boxer's right arm while the bomber is his straight left. And it is today a commonplace that a fighter force depends for its efficacy upon a first-class system of control and reporting. The gun also still has its place in an air defence system, especially light quick-firing weapons which are still of real value even against very high-speed aircraft, especially for the close defence of important points such as airfields against the very dangerous menace of low-flying attack. For other purposes the gun is approaching the end of its useful life and is already beginning to give way to the guided rocket.

But a simple calculation of radii of action, arcs of fire,

the range of early warning devices and the speed of attacking bombers, in relation to the size of the area to be defended, will reveal that to cover vast areas of country with an over-all defence even of modern fighters with their warning screens would mean that huge resources would have to be tied up for this purpose. We are fortunate in Britain in that we have a relatively small, compact zone to defend, though even in Britain we can not attempt to provide defence everywhere. It would be quite impracticable in the United States or Russia. It will always be a difficult task for any government to strike the happy mean in this respect and find the balance between the political and psychological factor and the military factor in the economics of air defence. Local politics must not be lightly overlooked in this respect, and this may be another advantage to the totalitarian state. There is a story about the late Field Marshal Sir William Robertson when he was Commandant of the Staff College at Camberley before the 1914-18 war. In a staff exercise designed to study the defence of Great Britain against invasion, a student decided to meet a threat to the south coast by withdrawing a unit from the Humber. "My boy, you've reckoned without the Mayor of Hull," said the Commandant. How right he was, as we frequently found in the late war. I remember the Director of Operations (Home) [8] at the regular Air Staff meeting in the old Air Council room one morning, when asked by the Vice Chief whether he had anything to report from the previous day, replying, "No, Sir, nothing of any importance, but one of these 'Baedeker' raiders came in and dropped half a dozen Parliamentary Questions in East Anglia." The Mayor of Hull and the local M.P. or Congressman will always be with us. It is a tough job to educate the civil population to

[8] Now Air Marshal Sir John Whitworth Jones.

understand that they can not all be given protection, but it can be done, as the people of Britain showed. When things are really bad the people's morale is greatly sustained by the knowledge that we are giving back as good as we are getting, and it engenders a sort of combatant pride, like that of the charlady in a government office who was asked during the London blitz where her husband was—"he's in the Middle East, the bloody coward!" We must ensure that defence, as adequate as we can reasonably make it, is afforded to those areas or installations which are really vital to our survival at the outset of a war, or to our ability to nourish our essential fighting strength. Much-Binding-in-the-Marsh and Littleville, Pa., are not in that category unless they happen to contain some utterly indispensable installation, and the inhabitants must steel themselves to risks and take what may come to them, knowing that thereby they are playing as essential a part in the country's defence as the pilot in the fighter or the man behind the gun.

Methods of air defence will certainly change. Some day perhaps we may see real push-button warfare and the end of the fighter as we know it today. That, I think, is one of the uncertainties which discourage some forward-looking boys from adopting the air force as a career. I don't think they need worry. At least some manned fighters will be with us for many years to come, and I can not visualize the disappearance of air crews from the air forces of the world in the foreseeable future.

One last word about defence: do not let us fall into the error of basing our thinking entirely on earlier wars. We need not dream up all sorts of bizarre nightmares, but a Communist enemy especially may adopt new and deadly forms of attack. We must be on our guard against such

possibilities as submarine-launched atomic rockets, sabo-
tage with chemical or biological agents and the "Trojan
horse" in our ports—the innocent-looking vessel with an
atomic bomb in her hold. Some of these things are extremely
difficult to guard against and we must have a care not to
waste resources on them. That brings us back again to the
first, the essential conclusion that, today more than ever
before, attack is the soul of defence.[9] We must prevent
this thing happening. And if it is forced upon us, we must
be able instantly to deliver a crushing counterattack upon
aggression at its source—not merely at its airfields, its
launching sites and submarine bases or its armies in the
field, but at the heart of the aggressor country. There will
be the battlefield, if battlefield there must be.

Of other elements of air power one can only say that
our needs should be conditioned by the strategy heretofore
outlined and by the sort of wars we may yet have to fight.
It should be possible to find further economies in some directions. I have already suggested that the scientific development of ground weapons may relieve tactical air forces
of some commitments, and I see no case for heavy expenditure on transport-support aircraft for airborne forces. Of
the R.A.F., it would be an overstatement to claim that
either Coastal Command or the transport force is fully
adequate to our reasonable needs, and it is difficult to see
how in present circumstances we could cut our already ex-
iguous strength in the Middle and Far East. In the United
States I suspect there are further economies to be found,
more particularly in the direction of a far higher degree of
unification of the multiple air forces to which I have al-

---

[9] "One element of our strength should indeed be ready and straining
at the leash. That is the retaliation force." Vannevar Bush, *Modern Arms
and Free Men*, Simon and Schuster, 1949.

ready referred. But it would be an impertinence for me to say more on that subject than I have already written, and no doubt there are many wise men in America far better qualified than I to say where further savings could be found without unacceptable loss of fighting value.

IV

In an earlier chapter I suggested that this generation may see more relatively small, localized wars such as that we have just gone through in Korea, and defined certain broad strategic principles applicable to that sort of war. There is no suggestion that we should or could ever have forces specially maintained and organized for "small wars." If they happen, we shall have to draw on our strategic reserves for the forces we need, and this sort of war, to judge by Korea, will call for standards of equipment and training not inferior to those required for real major war. So the dog we keep to deal with the cat, so to speak, will be able to deal with the kittens. And the lessons of Korea, particularly in so far as they relate to air power in the realm of what has been called battlefield strategy, are worth a glance, since they should influence our organization and training, not only for other "Koreas" of the future but for a possible great war.

I have already pointed out that in another small war we could not count upon the same degree of immunity from enemy air action that we enjoyed in Korea.[10] To that extent experience in Korea is most misleading in relation to the early stages of any kind of future war. We British are more fortunate (if that is the right way of putting it) than

---

[10] Except, of course, the aircrews who had to penetrate the defences of the enemy's back areas.

our American opposite numbers in that so many of our senior commanders have had personal experience in Belgium in 1940, in Greece or Crete or in the early days in Malaya, of what it feels like to have to fight when your enemy has command of the air. In the U.S. service on the other hand, with the exception of a gallant few who endured the horrors of Corregidor or Bataan, hardly any American general has any experience of fighting except when his own side enjoys almost complete air mastery. After all, from Alamein onwards the *Luftwaffe* was little more than a nuisance, quite a serious nuisance occasionally, but never a factor to be taken really seriously in a battle on land. And then in Korea the enemy presented us with this artificial situation of complete air superiority once again. That not only meant that our own back areas, with their airfields, communications, ports and depots, were immune from air attack, but it also led land-force commanders to expect far more lavish close air support than they have a hope of getting in any future war. Tactics and training improved in this respect after General Ridgway's arrival, but in the earlier days of open warfare the lightest opposition too often resulted in the troops diving for the nearest cover, reaching for the walkie-talkie set and demanding air support—and staying there till the air had dealt with the opposition.

As a general rule I think it is fair to say that when we remembered and applied the tactics and techniques that we—the British and Americans—evolved with blood, sweat, toil and tears in the North African desert, in the mountains of Italy, in the Normandy *bocage* or on the German plains, we didn't go far wrong. When we ignored or forgot them, then it cost us dear and we got surprises which should not have been a surprise to us at all. In the early days air force and army alike had forgotten much of the technique of co-operation which did us so well in World War II—things like the control of close support, filtering requests for air action and not using expensive aircraft to do what artillery could perfectly well do; the result was not only much initial inefficiency and a continuing waste of effort and life, but a resurgence of the silly bickering about the army having its own private air force, like the U.S. Marines, which to some extent embittered inter-service relations and again led to waste of effort. The army forgot how to combine fire and movement, got jeep-bound and ignored some simple tactical precepts which, if they were not within their own experience, they could well have learnt from their Allies. For instance in the early stages we heard a lot about "infiltration" by the North Koreans getting in behind United Nations units and shooting them up from the rear. It was perfectly plain to anyone with experience of the Indian frontier that what our commanders were doing was pushing along the valleys without picketing the high ground on their flanks—neglect of an elementary rule of mountain warfare which would have cost any *havildar* in the old Indian Army his stripes. I do not want to stray into the field of tactics, but the point is that in a close permanent alliance like ours, we should be quicker to learn from each other and not always have to buy our experience with human lives.

It was ignorance of another perfectly well-known lesson of World War II that led to some criticism of the air forces and much bewilderment at the enemy's ability to sustain his resistance—and even to make a number of quite serious local offensives—in the face of overwhelming air superiority and almost continuous interdiction of his communications in Korea. Just after the capture of Rome in

June 1944, General Marshall and General Arnold [11] were visiting Allied Force Headquarters in Italy, and they asked me for my views on the extent to which air power had contributed to the success of the recent operations. I gave them a little note, from which the following is an extract: "At the beginning of March he [the enemy] had substantial reserves in his depots and forward dumps, accumulated during the bad winter weather when flying was impossible for days on end and, in spite of the devastation of his communications and transportation, he was able, by superb organization and unremitting labour, to trickle forward a daily tonnage adequate to maintain his forward stocks well above the danger level *so long as he was not being forced to fight*. It must be remembered that, except for the short and abortive battle of Cassino in March, the Italian front was inactive from the close of the enemy's last attempt to drive in the beachhead [at Anzio] late in February till the opening of Diadem on 12 May. In these circumstances it proved impossible for the air to do more than hold the position on the enemy's supply front and pave the way for the joint offensive in May, by preventing the enemy from putting himself in a position to resist for a longer time than the Allies were in a position to continue attacking." [12] I quote this note at some length because I think it brings out a point of first-rate importance in the battlefield strategy of land-air warfare. The terrain of Korea with its few railways has something in common with that of Italy, and for about two years after the start of the armistice negotiations the armies were not fighting seriously, except in short

[11] Then Chiefs of Staff of the U.S. Army and the U.S. Air Force respectively.

[12] *Journal of the Royal United Service Institution*, Vol. XCIII, No. 570, May 1948.

and sometimes violent spasms. It might have been realized that air action against the communications and back areas of an enemy army can not have a decisive effect unless that army is being forced to *fight* [13]—to *expend* ammunition, fuel, engineer stores and spare parts and perhaps above all to move reserves, which can then be attacked, delayed and disorganized to a fatal degree, as was the well-known Hermann Goering Division by the time the remains of it eventually reached Valmontone in the battle for Rome. It is too early yet to see clearly how the tactical atomic weapon may affect this principle, but it may well remain true that the air force can not be really effective unless the army is fighting and it can then "make it impossible for the most highly organized and disciplined army to offer prolonged resistance to a determined offensive on the ground," [14] to quote the contemporary note again.

From this arises a related point that deserves the most thoughtful attention of those who are charged with the organization and training of the armies of the Free World. We must face the fact that our enemies in any kind of future war, whether they be Russian troops or (still more) those of their Asiatic partners, are inherently less vulnerable to air action, because they live and fight on a much more austere basis than the armies of the democratic powers and particularly of the United States. Troops who can live and fight on little more than a few grains of rice a day, supplemented by what they can loot from an already ruined countryside, are far less dependent on supply trains and truck convoys, rest camps and hospitals than those who find things like cigarettes and newspapers, Red Cross comforts, Coca-Cola and doughnuts essential to their existence.

[13] J. C. Slessor, *Air Power and Armies*, Oxford, 1936, p. 213.
[14] *Journal of the Royal United Service Institution, op. cit.*

I know an army is only a reflection of the nation from which it is drawn, and we can not expect our men to put up with a standard of living that would be a commonplace, or even a luxury, to a North Korean or a Chinese peasant soldier. But history shows that we can live tough and fight tough when we have to; so, while accepting the luxuries when we can get them, let us recognize them as the military handicaps they are and train our men to be hard when they have to be. These small wars when they come may well be in difficult country and unaccustomed climates. We should take all the advantage we may of air support and armour, helicopters and atomic artillery and all the rest of it. But the greatest need in Korea was, and will be again in other small wars, for tough, self-reliant infantry—men who can endure climatic hardships, march as their grandfathers marched with Sherman through Georgia or with Nicholson through the Punjab, dig like badgers and shoot like King's prize winners and eat like their enemies when they have to.

In writing of the lessons of Korea one must resist the temptation to get involved in the many interesting matters of detail, but there are two major points which we should take to heart in considering our future strategy for possible small wars, and indeed for any sort of war. First, it was a well-established fact long before 1950 that the air can not hold like an army in a prepared defensive position. Consequently in land-air warfare just as in a campaign between great air forces, the air must have depth for defence. That is to say it must have plenty of room behind the enemy's forward troops in which to make its weight felt against their communications and system of supply, and against the movement of their reserves. In a book published in 1936 I wrote: *"The aeroplane is not a battlefield weapon—the air striking force is not as a rule best employed in the actual*

zone in which the armies are in contact." [15] That is as true
today as eighteen years ago. One of the strongest reasons
for my dislike at the time of our advance to the Yalu in
1950 was that to do so would deprive the United Nations
armies of the massive support of air power, unless we were
prepared to spread the war into Manchuria, which for political reasons we were not prepared to do (whether or not
those political reasons were good, is irrelevant to this military point). And I am on record as being sure, when our
armies were subsequently in retreat towards the thirty-
eighth parallel, that as soon as they had come back far
enough to restore to us the depth in the enemy's rear to
enable the air to act freely again, the effect would be to
retard and finally to arrest the Communist advance. We
can not afford in our battlefield strategy to ignore the fact
that war on land today is land-air warfare—which is only
one of a number of reasons why a land-force general is by
no means necessarily always the best selection for the highest command in a campaign of this nature.

Finally, had the United Nations not possessed in Japan
a ready-made base reasonably close to the theatre of operations, it could hardly have been possible to make the rapid
concentration of land and air forces that, even so, only just
averted the speedy conquest of the whole peninsula by the
Communist armies. But here again do not let us forget
that the base in Japan was never subjected to air attack.
We must have actual or potential main bases somewhere
in the vicinity of areas in which we may have to fight. The
real essentials of a main base are communications (including, of course, ports and docks, rails and roads and airfields),
a reasonable stockpile of essential first-line equipment and
stores, and adequate supply of local labour and the depth

[15] Slessor, *op. cit.*, p. 90.

in front of it for defence. Even for another major war—and still less for one of our possible future "Koreas"—we do not need vast installations and dumps capable of nourishing scores of divisions and hundreds of squadrons. In any event, the nature and layout of bases today must take a form very different to what we have been accustomed to in the past, because a main base would be such an important objective for our enemy as fully to justify the use of atomic weapons.

Chapter 6

Air Power and the Problem of Europe

The great issue of policy which now confronts us is how we propose to solve the problem of the partition of Germany and of Europe. . . . the unity of Germany and the unity of Europe are inseparable.

Walter Lippmann, *Isolation and Alliances: An American Speaks to the British.*

For the last fifty years and more the problem of Germany has lain at the heart of Europe. It still does, perhaps more so today than ever before, divided as Germany is between the two great power blocs. We have always held that Germany should be reunited.

The Rt. Hon. Anthony Eden, P.C., M.P., Broadcast on 11 January 1954.

I

The leading statesmen of the Free World have repeatedly emphasized the pre-eminent importance of German unity in the solution of Europe's problems. At their conference in Washington in July 1953 the Foreign Ministers of Great Britain, the United States and France, referring to "the overwhelming desire of the German people to see unity established in freedom," expressed themselves as being confirmed in their view that "the early reunification of Germany, in accordance with the legitimate aspirations of the German population, would be a great contribution to the easing of international tension." This view was confirmed at Bermuda, and German unity is the major item on the agenda for the Four Power Conference in Berlin, of which the preliminaries are being arranged as these words are written. There are today few who deny the importance of this ideal or willingly accept the partition of Germany and the potentially explosive situation in Berlin as permanent features of the European scene, and not many who still blind themselves to the inevitability of German rearmament in some shape or form; but one may perhaps be excused the reflection that there seem to be far fewer who have really thought out the full implications of the first, or faced them in the context of the second. In fact it seems hardly an exaggeration to say that if by any strange chance we suddenly found ourselves tomorrow presented with this blessing for which we so devoutly pray, we should not know what on earth to do with it. It is unsafe to comfort ourselves with the reflection that it won't happen anyway, so we need not really worry. It will happen some day. It might happen much sooner and more unexpectedly than we think; it might suit the Russians much better than they now appear to believe. And anyway it is a fallacy to regard Russian foreign policy as an immensely long-term Machiavellian master plan. It has in fact been almost unbelievably stupid in the past and the Kremlin is liable to do unexpected things not as master strokes of policy but out of sheer stupidity. It has been well said: "Is it not possible that the Kremlin leaders seem vacillating and in two minds because they *are* vacillating and in two minds? The Emperor Napoleon III was for years reputed to be the most astute diplomatist in Europe because no one ever knew what he was going to do next—precisely, as it afterwards turned out, because he himself never knew what he was going to do next." [1] That sort of thing is not really a much better substitute for diplomacy than exasperation at the intransigence of an opponent or the hesitations of a friend. What would really confound the Free World in this political warfare with the Soviets is if *we ourselves* never knew what we are going to do next, which looks uncommonly like being our position in this matter of German unity. And one at least of the main reasons for our being in that position is that our political thinking, particularly that of our French partners, is based on an obsolete conception of strategy, and a failure to realize the decisive strength of the weapon we have in our hands as a solvent of some of Europe's oldest ills.

No British officer who has been through the two wars against Germany can have many delusions about the potential danger of Germany, and we have recently been sharply reminded of the perils inherent in a revival of old-fashioned German militarism.[2] I am not among those who are convinced that the German leopard never changes his spots and that it is still true that the German is always either at your throat or at your feet, and I believe Dr. Adenauer and his followers may be able to turn Germany into a staunch and stable member of the community of free peoples. Nevertheless it is merely silly to ignore the fact that a very real and justifiable fear of resurgent German militarism has long bedevilled the relations between Ger-

---

[1] "Observer," *The European Review*, December 1953.
[2] See *The Nemesis of Power*, by J. W. Wheeler-Bennett and *Sword and Swastika* by Telford Taylor.

many and her neighbours east and west—indeed all European relations—and will continue to do so unless the combined wisdom of Western statesmanship can find some way of healing that ancient sore and, above all, of achieving real reconciliation between Germany and France, lacking which European unity is no more than a dream. The Free World owes a great debt to Robert Schuman and Jean Monnet for the conception and initiation of the European Coal and Steel Community, which is an invaluable beginning in the vital economic sphere. It is far less certain that an attempt to impose the same sort of cure for a very different disease is the wisest or indeed at all a feasible solution in the military field. In any event it would be unlikely in itself to answer the question about a unified, rearmed Germany, and it is my object in this concluding chapter to put forward certain considerations which may help towards a solution of the supremely critical problem of reconciling European security with the rearmament of Germany.

II

At first sound, those last words may have a strange ring since the case for German rearmament has been primarily that European security is impossible without it. That, however, is the more immediate case of the defence against Russian invasion of a Western Europe in which Western Germany has been assumed, usually but not always tacitly, to be a sort of junior partner in the firm. Defence against Russia remains, and I believe will remain unless and until there is a complete change in the political complexion of the governing régime in Moscow, the dominating necessity, but it is far from being the whole problem. The real difficulty is that of reconciling the need for powerful German participation in the defence of the West with the assurance to France that a Germany in a different mood, and under less wise guidance than that of Dr. Adenauer, will not herself become the menace from the East—for the fourth time in a century. It was that dilemma which originally gave birth to the idea of a European Defence Community—a most peculiar baby at birth, which few people thought could ever develop into the slightly sturdier child it has now become. However, it has yet to prove itself capable of growing up into a reasonably healthy adult.

The actual need for any German rearmament is hardly worth discussing, but as it is still sometimes challenged it deserves a passing glance. It is in no spirit of resigned fatalism that I suggest it can really be summed up in the words of the old coloured preacher, "Ah doesn't try to know de unknowable; Ah doesn't attempt to unscrew de inscrutable; Ah just co-operates with the inebitable." The idea, popular in some quarters, of a "neutralized" Germany lying unarmed between the Eastern and Western camps can be dismissed as making no sense whatever. A limited rearmament of Germany first took its place in military thinking as a result of a mathematical calculation based on a sort of modernized version of World War II, which arrived at the result that x divisions were required to defend Western Europe and, since the N.A.T.O. partners could not see their way to raising more than y, therefore $x - y$ must be created by arming Germans. Q.E.D. There was also, of course, the political consideration that American and British public opinion could not be expected indefinitely to stand for the sacrifices necessary to defend Germany while the Germans themselves did nothing about it, but on the contrary busied themselves, free from military burdens, in undercutting us in the export markets of the world. It may be argued that on the new strategic basis advocated in this book German divisions are no longer so essential. Actually that argument is not tenable, as I have tried to show in an earlier chapter. There must be adequate strength on the ground in Germany, and at present there is not. German divisions and squadrons will no doubt ultimately have to relieve Allied forces in Germany; for the present they are required to supplement them. That, however, is not really the essential point. The fact is that it is fantastic to imagine that a strong, virile people like the Germans will remain indefinitely unarmed, surrounded on all sides by French and Belgians and Dutchmen, Poles and Czechs, all armed to the teeth. Germany is already *de facto* and will soon be *de jure* a sovereign state, and the right, indeed the duty, of self-defence is inalienable to any sovereign state, as Dr. Adenauer pointed out in his speech in Paris in December. I can hear the prophets of doom declaiming that we said all that last time when Germany was disarmed after the 1914-18 war, and look what happened! But even if the Germans have not changed—and it would be strange if they had not, after their experiences in the last thirty years—circumstances have; it is quite absurd to compare 1954 with 1924. So let us examine the European problem objectively against the background that German rearmament in some form is one of the facts of life.

I may be proved a false prophet before this book even sees the light of day, but I will take a chance on that and say that I shall be very surprised if the French ratify the E.D.C. agreement, and even if the treaty does succeed in scraping through the Assembly, it will still not be certain that the community with its supra-national authority and integrated international forces will in fact materialize. Originally a French concept, it was ludicrously impracticable in its initial form, but has since been so modified and tailored by practical people that it is not inconceivable that it might be made to work, after much initial creaking and groaning, if its constituent members were really loyally determined to make it do so. I say not inconceivable because I do not think anyone can rate its chances higher than that, composed as it would be of human beings of six different nationalities with human, and not ignoble, loyalties and traditions and prejudices—"can one pool men, and patriotic men at that, in the same way as one can pool knobs of coal?" [3] Englishmen, who are themselves rightly determined to do more than try from the outside to help its members make it work but in no circumstances to participate in it themselves, should not blame Frenchmen for jettisoning their ill-conceived baby. And the French have certainly no right to make out, as some do, that the failure of the E.D.C. to materialize can be laid at the door of the British refusal to participate. What the French can legitimately be blamed for is their lack of any constructive idea of a workable alternative, for their refusal to face direct German participation in N.A.T.O. and for all this nonsense about a "third force," the "neutralization" of Germany and so on. M. Bidault himself has said in the Assembly, "It is within our power to prevent the E.D.C., to prevent Germany from joining N.A.T.O. and even to prevent other matters. But it is possible that in consequence of the use which we shall have made of all our powers, we may be unable to prevent the failure of the E.D.C. from causing a crisis in the Atlantic system itself."

One of the factors contributing to French hesitations about the E.D.C. and their perfectly understandable fears about their future in Europe generally may perhaps be com-

[3] John Eppstein in the *British Survey*, December 1953.

pared to the feelings of a rather nervous member of a troupe of lion tamers who, having previously been badly mauled, is not unnaturally reluctant to be left alone in the cage with the lion—he may be a noble animal, at present amiably co-operating in the entertainment of the audience, but who knows that he will not lose his temper again? Many Frenchmen simply do not believe that British and American divisions and squadrons will remain indefinitely on Continental soil, and, to put it mildly, it is not unlikely that they are right—certain recent utterances in America will at least have lent some support to that view in France. I do not pretend to know what the policy of Her Majesty's Government or of the United States Administration is about this matter—or even if they have one. As far as I am aware there is no question of our coming away in the immediate or even near future. As a purely personal view, I find it extremely hard to believe that, whatever we may say now, British and American troops will in fact still be on the Continent in, say, ten years' time. I just do not think it is politically realistic to imagine that British, American and French forces will be stationed permanently on the soil of a sovereign Germany; indeed I do not see how the unity of Germany can be brought about without the evacuation of the Red Army, which we delude ourselves if we think possible without the simultaneous withdrawal of the Allied forces. The question therefore arises (and an answer is suggested later in this chapter)—if our forces are withdrawn, what do we put in their place? The mere fact that our obligations under N.A.T.O. bind us at least till 1969 are hardly likely, in the absence of a more immediately tangible safeguard, to allay the quite understandable fears of France that Germany may either seek to avenge 1945 or draw France into a war started by Ger-

many to regain the lost provinces, of which many thinking
Frenchmen seem more afraid than of direct attack. Frenchmen also fear the rise of Germany to a position of pre-
eminent influence in Europe—and in the E.D.C. if it were
to materialize—and that might well happen. But if it does,
it will be due almost as much to French political weakness
and internal dissensions as to Germany's inherent strength.
And anyway it could only be prevented either by a true
reconciliation between Germany and France—to which the
key is in French hands—or by the full participation of
Great Britain in a European political and military community, and it would be wrong to give the impression that
anything of the kind would ever be likely to receive the
support of British public opinion.

III

However, since we ourselves do not intend to join E.D.C.
we are not entitled to try to dissuade anyone who does from
going ahead with it if they think they can make it work
and, if it materializes, we should do our utmost to help.
For my part, I have in the past been less cautious and
more hopeful in this regard than some perhaps wiser
people, because I thought it was better than what looked
like being a possible alternative, the disruption of N.A.T.O.
But no friend of France should hesitate to point out the
difficulties and dangers in the E.D.C. idea. I have always
thought direct German participation in N.A.T.O. more
practical and in essence no more potentially dangerous to
France than the E.D.C.—indeed from a purely professional
military point of view no one in his senses who could get
the first would look at the second. But even that does not
alter the fact that either course has difficulties in relation

to the unification of Germany. Let us, therefore, in this context look first at that problem on the assumption that the E.D.C. has been ratified and put into effect, and then turn to consider whether there are other possible ways of meeting the immediate requirements of European defence which might provide France with the assurance she quite naturally demands, allay the fears of Russia (which are too real to be safely ignored) and at the same time put fewer difficulties in the way of German unity. Any course has its dangers. But the most dangerous may be simply to plod ahead on the E.D.C. road without adopting some constructive policy to put in its place in case it fails to materialize or breaks down subsequently, and without looking far enough ahead to see where it is leading us through the rough going towards German unity.

The advocates of the E.D.C., and for that matter of direct German participation in N.A.T.O., presumably take the view that it will be practicable in the reasonably near future for a sovereign, reunified Germany to come into being within the defence orbit of the West—they would obviously reject any idea of that being acceptable within the defence orbit of the East. Dr. Adenauer certainly holds that view; like Sir Winston Churchill he does not believe in looking too far ahead and he likes to jump one fence at a time—his immediate fence is to get the Federal Republic firmly tied in with the E.D.C., on which he has staked his political position. He is unequivocal on the essential need for German unity but believes, and not without good reason, that he has as strong support in the Soviet zone of Germany as in the Federal Republic for his policy of military integration with western Europe. His assumption is that the Kremlin respects nothing but strength and in due course (sooner than most people imagine) will give

way to the extent of relaxing its grip on Eastern Germany
and allowing it to be won over to a unified Reich, in which
the Federal Republic will already be inextricably committed to the defence system of the West by its participation in E.D.C.

Now, if that really is likely to be a practical possibility,
it would obviously suit us admirably and we should do our
utmost to bring it about. But one sometimes misses the
bull's-eye just as far by setting his sights too high as setting
them too low. Let us be quite clear what it means—namely
that in the reasonably near future there is a real prospect
of Soviet Russia agreeing to one of her satellites, the (to
her) valuable and potentially dangerous Eastern Germany,
throwing off her allegiance to Moscow, liquidating the indigenous agents of the Kremlin who now misrule her and
openly joining the North Atlantic Alliance,[4] which Malen-
kov and Co. never tire of branding as an offensive coalition aimed at Russia. One surely need not be a great ad-
mirer of the wisdom or consistency of Soviet policy to find
it somewhat difficult to accept that anything quite as simple
as that is likely in the near future. Walter Lippmann says,
"We can not evacuate Germany if Germany has not become bound by her own sovereign choice and action within
a European system"—by which he presumably means a
European defence system. Is it not at least likely that
Russia would find it equally impossible if Germany *were*
so bound? It may be true that Russia is more threatened
by internal dissensions, by critical shortages of food and
by the malevolent dislike of her satellite subjects than we
commonly think—the men of Bonn, with their window
on the East and their thousands of recently returned pris-

[4] The E.D.C. forces are intended to be under the command and at
the disposal of S.H.A.P.E.

oners of war, may have better grounds than we on which to base a judgment. Those factors may be strong enough to induce Moscow to evacuate the Red armies on terms less unacceptable to the West than anything the Russians have previously shown any signs of being willing to consider, but I find it hard to visualize them accepting without any balancing advantage the loss of two on a division, so to speak—giving up one of their satellites with its natural resources and seeing the N.A.T.O. forward line, reinforced by German units, move forward at one bound to the Oder and the Neisse. Is that not to underestimate the fear complex in Soviet policy? Dr. Adenauer does not believe that fear is genuine and asks how Russia, with her vast resources and enormously greater manpower can really be afraid of Germany. With respect to a wise old man, I think he takes too simple a view of that, and if I were a Russian I should look with anything but confidence on the possibility of being attacked by Germany again, particularly if I believed (as I should if I were a Russian Communist) that Germany would have behind her the might of N.A.T.O.

In any event, I am sure Dr. Adenauer would not suggest that German unity is likely to come about by that means alone for some years at least, and it might be a long time. Meanwhile we remain faced with what Walter Lippmann has called "a grave predicament—that the strategic interests of the Atlantic Community, as we now conceive them and as we are now developing them, will come into direct collision, not only with the purposes of our great adversary, the Soviet Union—but also with the national interests of the German people." [5] Is it not indeed true

[5] *Isolation and Alliances: An American Speaks to the British*, Little, Brown and Company, 1952.

that we may be leaving in the hands of the Kremlin a trump
card which it is quite unsafe to assume they would not
play if and when it suited them? And they may come to
the conclusion, earlier than we think, that it *would* suit
them. Let us look for a moment at how the Russians *may*
be beginning to view the situation in Europe today.

The Kremlin's aim has been the antithesis of our own—
to secure the domination, by cold war methods or by hot,
of the rich resources of Western Europe, as a first step to
their crazy nirvana of a Communist world dominated by
Moscow. They have probably given up the idea of doing
it by the old-fashioned method of military conquest. They
may now be coming to the view either that time is on their
side and they can play a long-term waiting game, or that
their best bet is to do it by the more subtle Communist
methods of subversion, of rotting their enemies' defences
from the inside, in which the first and most obvious step
is to disrupt the unity of N.A.T.O. and prevent the further
integration of Western Europe. I suppose it is not inconceivable that they have at last realized that their own great
natural resources are ample for their own growing population, if only they would devote more attention to developing them instead of making a nuisance of themselves to
other people, but perhaps it is too much to hope for that
degree of elementary common sense in a Communist.
Anyway, there are good grounds for the belief that they
now realize that their earlier policy of holding the blunder-
buss of 175 divisions and thousands of aircraft at the head
of the Free World has failed; it merely brought N.A.T.O.
into being and hastened the atomic rearmament of the
United States and Great Britain. They still feel the need,
perhaps more than ever, for depth for their own defence
against the attack by the capitalist world, which their

crazy creed tells them is bound to come. They may have correctly concluded that German rearmament is inevitable anyway, and may think either that "a united, armed and unbound Germany would have everything to gain by renewing the old alliance with Russia," [6] or that, if they must face the possibility of a future attack by Germany, it would be in their interest to do everything possible to ensure that they have to face Germany alone and not as a partner in N.A.T.O. All this may be adding up to the view that on balance it would pay them—if only for the disruptive effect it would have on N.A.T.O.—to withdraw their forces from Germany on terms, in the knowledge and on the condition that to do so would certainly mean that Great Britain and the United States would have to do the same. After all, they would merely be withdrawing the Red Army a few hundred miles across land frontiers, whence it would be easier for them to return if they wanted to than for the British and Americans to come back across the Channel and the Atlantic. The Kremlin might even conclude, perhaps under pressure from the Red General Staff, that the interests of their own security would be better served by a *cordon sanitaire* of neutral, even if not very friendly, buffer states—a sort of extension of Sweden southwards to the Black Sea—than by having to continue to hold down in the satellite states of Eastern Europe about a hundred million people, almost all of whom loathe the sight of them. Very unlikely, it may be said, it would mean accepting what would amount to a major defeat in the cold war. I do not suggest it as very likely, but Russian foreign policy, however inept it may sometimes be, has at least the advantage of being conducted without sentiment, and it is anyway not impossible that the Kremlin might

[6] *Ibid.*

think that what they would stand to gain west of the present Iron Curtain would offset their losses to the east of it. Having the bear by the tail is not a comfortable position to be in at the best of times, but if you can contrive at the same time to kick him on the snout it may be safe to let go, and they may reckon—and perhaps rightly—that they have sufficient brute force to offset in the other satellites the loss of prestige which might result from the course of action envisaged.

I do not suggest this as being the least likely in the immediate future—the Soviet note of 3 November 1953 does not look much like it. At the Berlin Conference in a couple of weeks' time the Russians will probably make another attempt to fob off German rearmament and to throw monkey wrenches into the unity of the Western Allies. But it is far from impossible that at some future date they may take advantage in some way of the initiative we shall have left with them, to try to disrupt N.A.T.O. That might even take the form of an offer to the Federal Republic to withdraw the Red Army (on condition, of course, that British, American and French forces also withdraw) and recognize a sovereign, unified Reich, with no other strings [7] except that this unified Reich should be free from all military entanglements and the present Soviet zone be demilitarized. This might be

[7] It seems unlikely that the "lost provinces" beyond the Oder-Neisse line would figure at all in any Soviet offer to Germany. If they had brought themselves to making an offer to Germany on the lines envisaged, it would not be worth their risking its rejection by including a condition that Germany should ratify the Potsdam frontier (the Allies would surely bring no pressure to bear to that end). And, though they would not hesitate to betray the Poles if they thought it suited them, it seems unlikely that they would invite the inevitable violent hostility in Poland that would result from an offer to Germany to support the restoration of the lost provinces, at the same time as they were taking the risk of withdrawing their troops from Germany.

coupled with an immediate offer of arms, including tanks
and fighter aircraft. They have said something not unlike
that in the past—suppose they say it again, and this time
really mean it? Might not such an offer be difficult for any
German government to refuse? Dr. Adenauer apparently
does not think so. But he will not be there for ever, and
in point of fact I wonder whether even he would be strong
enough to hold the position, if the alternative were an indefinite prolongation of Soviet occupation of the Eastern
Lander, and no doubt intensified pressure on the unfortunate population. The Eastern Germans certainly favour
his policy now, but it is far from certain that they would
continue to do so, if it looked like resulting in an indefinite
continuation of their ordeal under Soviet rule. The Germans may like the idea of the E.D.C. now, when they are
disarmed and helpless, for the same reason they welcome
the presence in Germany of British, American and even
French forces *now*, but would they continue to do so when
there are German forces in existence and if it looked as
though it was only the presence of Allied troops in Western
Germany that was keeping the Red Army in the East? It
would be all very well for their government and the Allies
to tell them to be patient and the Russians will tire of it
and go anyway; the Russians might well show no signs of
weakening, and the feeling would grow in Germany, fostered by Soviet propaganda, that it was the Allies who
were keeping them there for our own selfish ends by refusing to evacuate the Allied troops. Moreover there would
be Germans—and their numbers would grow—who would
not be insensible of the imagined joys of being the real
political and strategic makeweight in Europe, throwing
their influence now on the side of the West, now on that
of the East, as it suited them.

It is no doubt true that the present Federal government would be strong enough to refuse such an offer, certainly if it were made in present circumstances. Another future government of the Federal Republic might not find it impossible to refuse, and would certainly find it more difficult to accept as members of E.D.C., which, of course, may be an argument for going ahead with that organization. But membership of E.D.C. would not make it impossible for a future government of Germany, in circumstances which may be different from those today, to accept an offer on these lines; E.D.C. in the form into which it has developed is not an omelette which could not be unscrambled; still less is N.A.T.O. So it in fact offers the French a more slender safeguard than they appear to think. In fact the more difficult Germany's prospective partners try to make it for Germany to break away, by an undue insistence on points like her exclusion from the North Atlantic Council, the prohibition of a German General Staff and the limitation of her armaments (the last two of which history shows can not be effective if Germany is determined they shall not be), the more they exacerbate that feeling of inferiority which many Germans already resent, and thus weaken the bonds of any defence community. We are in a dilemma which we can not evade by pretending it does not exist. We can go ahead with E.D.C. or with direct German participation in N.A.T.O. (and in relation to the really critical problem there is not much to choose between the two) in the hope that German reunification may come about in the way Dr. Adenauer hopes, which, if I am right, is unlikely, at least for a long time to come. But that alone is not good enough. It is clearly unwise to try to find a neat solution for every conceivable situation far in advance. But there are limits to this policy of jumping the first fence first and hoping for the best—it sometimes leads to a very nasty fall. No sensible jockey goes down to the start without knowing anything about the course except the first fence, and one looks to a different horse to jump the Grand National course to the one that would do very well for a small selling steeplechase—the former may be a much less pleasant ride but the latter won't survive really big fences. In jumping this E.D.C. fence we should at least have our eyes open to the possibility that it may before long involve accepting one of two alternatives—either that German unification results from a Soviet initiative, coupled with a breach of faith by some future Federal government, which we could in fact do nothing to prevent, or that it is indefinitely postponed by the refusal of a Federal government to fall for the Russian initiative, leading to prolonged partition of Germany with all the dangers and difficulties involved, including the indeterminate prolongation of the presence of British and American forces on European soil. Another no more agreeable and perhaps more likely possibility is that no such Soviet initiative as I have envisaged will be forthcoming, and that the assumption that Russia will relax her grip on Eastern Germany within a reasonable period turns out to be a delusion. That, apart from the more obvious disadvantages and dangers of perpetuating a Russian frontier on the Elbe and the present position in Berlin, would, like the second alternative, incur the dangerous consequences of thwarting the overwhelming and perfectly legitimate desire of the German people for the reunification of their country. And any political or military arrangement calculated to increase the probability of that would indeed have to contain very cogent compensating advantages to be acceptable.

IV

In considering other possible methods of resolving this dilemma which either might be deliberately selected as an alternative to E.D.C. or we might have up our sleeve in case E.D.C. is not ratified or requires major modification after it has materialized, it is important to clear our minds as to the essential conditions that any defence arrangement must fulfil if it is to be acceptable. I suggest they can be defined as follows and they are not to be regarded as in any fixed order of priority though some are clearly more weighty than others; the importance of some may increase and of others recede as circumstances change, but in essence they must all be fulfilled.

Any arrangement:

1. Must provide at least as effectively as the present E.D.C.-N.A.T.O. concept for the defence of the Free World against Soviet aggression.
2. Must recognize that participation of the United States in the defence of Europe is vital. This means it must be of a nature likely to be acceptable in the long term to American public opinion.
3. Must hold out a reasonable prospect of making it possible for a sovereign, unified German state, which we have already assumed will be armed, to be established before too long.
4. Must, therefore, be such that in due course British, American and French forces can be withdrawn from Western and Russian forces from Eastern Germany. This can not be done prematurely, and certainly not before some Western Germans themselves are re-

armed; a partial withdrawal would not be acceptable. The idea of a withdrawal to the periphery leaving Berlin and an area of Central Germany free, while attractive in theory, is not really a practical proposition, and British and American forces could not in practical fact be withdrawn to France and the Benelux countries while the Russians are withdrawn to Poland and Czechoslovakia. When the occupying forces are ultimately evacuated the Russians must withdraw to Russia and the British and Americans from the Continent.

5. Must be such as to give reasonable assurance to the French against the possibility of another German military domination of Europe, and ultimately lead to a genuine Franco-German reconciliation, to which relatively minor details like the Saar should not be allowed to present an obstacle.

6. Must also take account of the hardly less understandable fears in Russia of resurgent German militarism, and in general must be of a nature that would be reasonably possible for the Kremlin to accept. I am aware that the Kremlin is not reasonable, but that is no excuse for us to be the same and produce some solution which it would be quite unrealistic for us to expect Moscow to agree to, such as the immediate detachment of Poland and Czechoslovakia from the Soviet bloc, the removal of Russian "advisers" and so on. This is not to suggest that the Kremlin will necessarily accept any arrangement in the sense of signing an agreement on the dotted line. I have already submitted that an arrangement with Communist governments should be in the nature of

a simple, formal notification and clarification of our intent, which they can take or leave as they like.

7. Must not prejudice the object of our strategy for the West as defined in Chapter 1 of this book— i.e. it must not affect adversely and if possible should improve the prospects of releasing the satellite states from the yoke of Moscow.

8. Must give united Germany assurance against aggression and some hope that her soil will not again become a battlefield.

9. Must create a situation leading to some peaceful solution by agreement of outstanding problems such as the Potsdam frontiers, and must make it clear that such problems can not safely be resolved by resort to armed force.

10. Must be binding for a period long enough to give a sense of stability and a chance for the world political weather to clear under its protection.

11. Finally, and this perhaps is a "should" rather than a "must"—a desideratum rather than an indispensable condition—any arrangement should face the fact that the Soviet and Western philosophies of life are likely to be incompatible for a very long time, and should aim at the setting up of some physical and political no man's land between the two blocs in Europe. To begin with, this might take the form of voluntary demilitarization by united Germany of the present Soviet zone when it is evacuated by the Red Army. And it seems not entirely unrealistic ultimately to envisage something on the lines of what I have already suggested, a chain of "Swedens" from Poland through Czechoslovakia and Hungary to Rumania and Bulgaria. The colour of their own

internal politics would be their own affair—if they want to be Communist, then let them be so like Yugoslavia. I suspect that in fact an early political development in most of the countries named would be a temporary decoration of the lampposts. They would, however, like Sweden, be allied neither to East nor West and bound by no pledges, but if attacked from East or West could count in practice upon the other side for support against the aggressor.

The fear that German rearmament will lead to another great war is natural and widespread, not only on the Continent but in Great Britain. Every town and village war memorial in our country has its tragic list of young men killed in the two great wars that have owed their origin to German aggression. What more natural than that there should be this legacy of suspicion and fear that to rearm Germany will only lead to the militarists once more getting the upper hand, and to another holocaust of youth? But that need not be so and to understand why, it is essential to be clear on a point which I think is far from commonly understood and which should be stated plainly at this stage, since it is fundamental in any truly objective appraisal of the military situation in Europe— indeed the assumption on which it is based is inherent in the whole theme of this book. It is that Germany can never again be a military menace to her neighbours if Great Britain and the United States remain determined that she shall not be. No one really understands air power who has not had to wield it. And the thinking of almost all European generals is governed by a disregard or denial of this basic military truth. To the French, the defence of France means

L'Armée Française, with a top-dressing of tactical air, and when they think of the German menace, they see in their mind's eye the *pickelhaubes* of Sedan and the Marne and the panzers of 1940. It should be obvious by now that I am far from ignoring the menace of great armies. But they are no longer the real crux of the matter of European defence against a menace from the East, whether it be the Red tide of today or the Grey tide of a conceivable tomorrow. The real factor that has brought into being this new situation, this basic military truth to which I have referred, is atomic air power. It may be difficult but we know it is not impossible for Anglo-American air power to reach out across the great spaces of Russia to the vital centres deep in the heart of that vast country. It would be too easy to do the same anywhere in Germany. I do not pretend to be an expert on German psychology, but every thinking German can surely remember great Allied bomber fleets, escorted by fighters, ranging at will over the length and breadth of his country in the face of one of the strongest air defence systems ever devised. They can still see in their shattered cities all too much remaining evidence of what that bomber offensive did to their country ten years ago. They must know—or, if they do not, the sooner they learn the better—that what it took us five years to do last time we could do, and much more, in five days another time, *and they could do nothing to prevent it*. I can not think it likely that Germany would ally herself with Russia against the West, but it is not inconceivable—she has done it before. But even if she did and whatever the ultimate issue of such a war, one thing about it is beyond question—Germany would emerge from it with her cities a mass of radio-active rubble and with millions of her people dead or terribly maimed. A horrible picture, but war is horrible and would be more than ever so in the future. For the Germans there would be another time no dazzling quick victories, no more succession of "lurid prizes" with the panzer divisions and the grey infantry sweeping over country after country under a sky aswarm with Stukas. Aggressive war would bring home to them retribution, swift, overwhelming and personal, *provided always* that we in the West, the two great democratic powers who have in their hands the terrible weapon of that retribution, do not throw it aside, disrupt our unity, relax our resolve and sink back into that same blind, selfish apathy that brought us to the brink of disaster fourteen short years ago. That the same awful fate might befall England and even the great cities of America is true but does not affect the issue. War in the future would be atomic, hydrogen war and would begin, as Sir Winston Churchill has said, by both sides suffering what they dread most. And to shrink from that dread prospect, to try to run away from our responsibilities and allow initial aggression, by whatever enemy, to go unchecked would only postpone for a short spell the evil day and make certain our defeat in the world war that would inevitably follow.

V

The heads of states assembled at Bermuda in December 1953 found it necessary to asssert that "the European Defence Community is needed to assure the defensive capacity of the Atlantic Community, of which it will be an integral part." If that statement was dictated by considerations of political expediency—by the feeling that to abandon or even fail to express support for the E.D.C. at Bermuda so soon before a Four Power Conference in Berlin might disrupt the Atlantic system, which was rightly

declared to be "the foundation of our common policy"—
then to that extent no doubt it was justified. But, with
great respect to the distinguished sponsors of the Bermuda
communiqué, from a military point of view the statement
will not hold water. On the contrary, the very existence of
the E.D.C. might prove actually to be a military stumbling
block in the path of "the continuing development of a
united Europe including Germany." The Berlin Conference
will be over by the time these words are printed, and it
is surely no longer a disservice to be frank about the E.D.C.
One of the many recent French governments some three
years ago was faced with the dilemma that to maintain their
violent opposition to German rearmament might lose them
the support of the United States in the defence of Europe.
To solve this dilemma they thought up, without any proper
professional examination, the project of a European Army
containing small German contingents dispersed amongst its
international divisions; this they imagined would assure
European security against a possible future aggression by
Germany, if the nature of the proposal did not result in
their Allies dropping the hot brick of German rearmament
altogether, which perhaps they hoped it would. The fact
that the concept has since been developed from the infantile
absurdity of the initial suggestion into something which
makes more sense, and might become a workable military
proposition if all its members were wholeheartedly and un-
selfishly determined that it should, does not alter or mini-
mize the disadvantages of the fact that the whole idea was
rushed through in an atmosphere of desperate urgency, to
putty up a gap in an Allied front which looked uncommonly
like crumbling in the face of what was then believed to be
serious danger, and that its full, long-term political and
military implications simply were not considered. Testing it

now objectively against the conditions suggested above as being essential to any sound military arrangement, making the very bold assumption that it could in fact be made to work, and giving it the benefit of the doubt under several heads, it may be said that it would fulfil conditions 1 and 2 and 5 onwards, but that it might put a serious obstacle in the way of 3 and hence of 4—might make German unity impossible in the foreseeable future—and might even be it-self disrupted by a future German withdrawal, which would certainly make a nonsense of condition 5, to which the French understandably attach such major importance.

"Needed to assure the defensive capacity of the Atlantic Community" means that our defensive capacity can not be assured without it, and that is quite definitely untrue. It might be one method, *faute de mieux*, of assuring the defensive capacity of the West, though there are anyway doubts about that. We should, however, at least be ready with some alternative which is built on less shaky founda-tions than E.D.C.

The most obvious and easy alternative, of course, is that Germany should become a full partner in N.A.T.O. on a footing of equality with the other fourteen member states. This would be far more efficient from the military and I should have thought more practical from the political point of view—it does not try to eat the whole cherry tree of supra-national sovereignty at one bite. Apart, however, from this, which means we know for sure it would be a workable military proposition, there is not much to choose between it and the E.D.C. in relation to my eleven condi-tions. It might be more difficult for the Russians to swal-low. But the main objection to it is that it is regarded by the French, and with some reason, as violating condition 5. It would obviously be easier for a future German gov-

ernment to break away from military association with the
West, and that possibility, however unlikely, is the whole
ground for French fears and hence the basis of the E.D.C.;
in fact it was to prevent direct German participation in
N.A.T.O. that M. Pleven produced the E.D.C. rabbit out
of his hat. In my own view the serious objection to this
course is that it would make German unity very difficult
to achieve, except in the (to me) unlikely circumstances
for which Dr. Adenauer hopes. But in any event, though
from a military point of view greatly preferable to E.D.C.,
there does not seem any reason to suppose that the French,
who would have to ratify German admission to N.A.T.O.,
would find it any more acceptable today than they did
three years ago.

An American solution put forward by Mr. Lippmann
about two years ago [8] involved Germany becoming firmly
committed to a European system, effecting a real reconciliation with France sealed by a treaty binding them to
concert their foreign policy in Europe (the E.D.C. does
not figure in this idea), and negotiating a settlement of the
common frontier dispute with Poland. Evacuation of the
occupying armies would then start, beginning with a withdrawal from the centre of Germany to the periphery. I
have already expressed my view that this last is not really
feasible, but it was perhaps not an essential part of the
idea, which was not meant to be a clear-cut plan but merely
stated in general terms certain conditions to be observed.
I doubt whether it would form the basis of any practical
arrangement today; the recent unhappily typical Polish reaction to Dr. Adenauer's suggestion of a Polish-German
condominium or United Nations trusteeship for the former

[8] *Isolation and Alliances: An American Speaks to the British*, Little,
Brown and Company, 1952.

German territories east of the Oder certainly bodes ill for the fulfilment of one of Mr. Lippmann's essential conditions.

A number of other suggestions for a solution of this problem have been aired, among the most recent of which was a scheme adumbrated by the British Society for International Understanding [9] on the following lines: Great Britain is committed by the Treaty of Brussels of 1948 to a mutual defence guarantee against external attack with four of the proposed E.D.C. states, France, Belgium, the Netherlands and Luxembourg—the old Western Union of Fontainebleau; the idea is that Germany should be invited to adhere to this treaty, thus extending the British guarantee to Germany on a reciprocal basis; a protocol of adherence could make provisions for the limitation of German armaments similar to those already accepted under the E.D.C. Treaty; Italy could be invited to join if she so desires; and Germany would have a seat in the revived Brussels Treaty Council of Ministers. It could be formally agreed that nothing would prevent any signatories of this treaty forming a political and military community within the treaty— in other words an E.D.C.—if they wanted to. The really important feature of this scheme derives from the wording of Article 4 of the treaty signed in Brussels on the seventeenth of March 1948: "If any of the Parties *should be the subject of an armed attack in Europe*, the other Parties will, in accordance with Article 51 of the United Nations Charter, afford the Party attacked all military and other aid and assistance in their power." The operative words, of course, are those italicized. The partnership of Western Union which was welded together by the Brussels Treaty and N.A.T.O. into which it subsequently developed have

[9] *The British Survey*, December 1953.

naturally concentrated their attention on the only possible immediate threat of armed attack in Europe, namely attack by Russia, and most people have probably forgotten that the wording of the Brussels Treaty was general and did not limit its application to the contingency of Russian attack. There is no reason why, if the Brussels Treaty were reaffirmed and extended, it should not spell out in specific terms that its obligations would apply to the case of attack by one signatory upon another—other treaties, such as that of Locarno, have included just that provision. That, if the treaty were extended as suggested, would of course apply to the case of attack by Germany on France at any future date within the lifetime of the treaty, and that would surely give an assurance to France of which the rejection would be beyond all reason. One must be prepared for the argument that such a pact could not be reconciled with N.A.T.O. and would not be acceptable unless the United States also adhered to the Brussels Treaty. I see no reason why it should conflict with N.A.T.O., which exists for a specific purpose—defence against Russian aggression —and is in fact the only thing which could give real effect to the provisions of Article 4 in respect of the most dangerous and least unlikely contingency, since it enlists on the side of the Brussels powers the immense support of the United States. Indeed, the authors of the scheme under discussion imply that it would lead inevitably to German admission to the North Atlantic Council, and to that France could hardly object if she had the assurance against future German aggression provided by the extended Article 4 of Brussels. It would probably mean the removal of the quantitative and qualitative limitations on German rearmament inherent in the E.D.C. scheme and accepted by the Federal government. That would have the advantage of removing a dangerous source of ill-will arising out of a feeling of inferior status on the part of the Germans, but also surely it is unrealistic to ignore the lessons of history in this regard. I would like to see Germany adhere permanently to an undertaking not to make or maintain atomic weapons or guided missiles, but can not convince myself that such a self-denying ordinance—still less prohibition—would stand the test of time; it seems to me that the only common-sense view to take is that a partnership can not survive unless it is an equal partnership, and you can not have one member of a club who is denied access to the card-room.

It might be argued in Paris that the provisions of the extended Brussels Treaty would not provide against the possibility of Germany at some future date provoking and getting France involved in a war to regain the lost territories in the East. That is a criticism of some substance. The democratic Germany of Dr. Adenauer is highly unlikely to embark on any such adventure. But that is not the Germany we have to fear; and the urge to regain the lost provinces is a more likely cause of a future war than any thirst for revenge on France. Actually, as I shall later suggest, I think provision could be made for a safeguard against it.

The point about United States participation is more substantial and is importantly connected with the one major difficulty in the scheme suggested by the British Society for International Understanding, namely that in itself it accords no more than E.D.C. or German participation in N.A.T.O. with the practical conditions likely to be necessary to secure the withdrawal of the armies of occupation, without which German reunification remains impossible. If that difficulty can not be solved, the scheme should not be rejected on that account, any more than by reason of the United States not adhering to it. If the United States (and Canada) would adhere, with Germany, to the Brussels Treaty, so very much the better, but it would be highly captious to condemn the scheme on the sole ground that it does not commit the United States to safeguard France against hypothetical German action in the remote future. Let us see, however, whether there is not some means by which we could reconcile this possible French objection with the far more vital requirement of restoring unity with freedom to Germany; a means which might appeal to the earnest desire of the people of the United States to find a way of solving the present impasse in Europe, and to which even the Russians might be unable indefinitely to oppose their usual bovine intransigence; a means finally which might enable the Atlantic Allies at last to take a constructive initiative in their dealings with the Soviet bloc.

VI

Let us restate the problem reduced to its simplest terms; it is to reconcile three essentials—the defence of Western Europe against Russian aggression, the establishment of unity with freedom in Germany and a safeguard against renewed German military domination of Europe, and to do it in such a way as to give no reasonable grounds for Russian fears.

Speaking in the House of Commons on the eleventh of May last year, the Prime Minister said that in considering this problem of Germany, the Treaty of Locarno of 1925 had been in his mind, a treaty "based upon the simple provision that if Germany attacked France, we should stand with the French, and if France attacked Germany we should stand with the Germans." [10] I do not know whether it was this that put the idea into the heads of the Social Democrats in the German elections that a reunited Germany should renounce all military alliances (including, of course, the E.D.C.) and rely on a system of mutual guarantee by the present occupying powers. They were not the only German political party to have some such idea. Dr. Adenauer himself suggested some sort of security guarantee, and he appears to have had in his mind something in the nature of a nonaggression pact between the E.D.C. and the Soviets. But any guarantee must be backed by some sanction, without which unfortunately no simple nonaggression pact or solemn undertaking between two powers or groups of powers is worth the paper it is written on. Russia would merely regard such a nonaggression pact as a useful tactical means of making ultimate aggression easier. On this side of the Iron Curtain neither France nor Germany would be satisfied with a mere obligation to "stand with them," or to afford them "all military and other aid and assistance in our power" without more specific safeguards. They might well remind us that we gave that sort of "guarantee" to Poland in 1939 and it meant nothing. The assumption is that the terms of any settlement must include the withdrawal of the armies of occupation from a unified Germany, which for the British and Americans means from Europe. Our Allies would point out, with unanswerable logic, that the Red Army might well overrun them before our forces could return to their aid, and they are not likely to be consoled by the thought that they would ultimately be liberated and avenged. So that any security guarantee or treaty on the Locarno model

[10] It is the principle that is important, not the details of the Locarno Treaty.

must be backed by some sanction that does not depend for its validity on the continued presence of British and American forces in Europe. It must at the same time involve a firm commitment to the effect that any aggressor would instantly be subjected to overwhelming force, of a nature that would almost certainly deter him from aggression and would at least bid fair to destroy him if he did attack.

And that sanction can only be air power. So my proposal is as follows:

1. The Treaty of Brussels should be superseded by another, on almost exactly similar lines and including Article 4 as at present drafted, which I suggest should be signed in Berlin. Its original signatories should be the Brussels Treaty powers with the addition of the Federal Republic of Germany, the United States and Canada.

2. The Berlin Treaty should include an article specifically providing for its application in the case of attack by one signatory power upon another.

3. If necessary in order to secure the agreement of the Congress of the United States, the life of the Berlin Treaty should be the same as that of N.A.T.O., with provision for its extension by agreement after 1969. If possible, however, its period should correspond with that of the Brussels Treaty—i.e. until 1998.

4. As soon as the Berlin Treaty is signed, we should invite Soviet Russia, Poland and Czechoslovakia to adhere to it, taking full advantage of its guarantees as well as undertaking its obligations. If they refuse— and Russia would almost certainly do so initially, compelling her satellites to do the same—the offer

would remain open. Meanwhile it would be made clear to the three Eastern states that as long as they stand apart from it they remain subject to its sanctions without enjoying its safeguards.

5. N.A.T.O. would remain in existence in its present form, except that on signature of the Berlin Treaty the Federal Republic would be invited to join it. The Berlin Treaty would have no military organization of its own, and N.A.T.O. would be as necessary as ever, to give effect to the provisions of the Berlin Treaty in the event of Soviet aggression.

6. Turkey, Greece, Italy and all the other members of N.A.T.O. would be free to adhere to the Berlin Treaty if and when they so desire, as also would Yugoslavia and Spain, though, of course, without becoming members of N.A.T.O.

7. As soon as the Berlin Treaty is ratified the North Atlantic Allies should inform Russia that as soon as the German forces considered necessary by N.A.T.O. have been organized and trained to the requisite standard, we propose to begin the progressive evacuation of British, American and other Allied forces from the soil of the Federal Republic, and should require Russia to withdraw her forces from the present Soviet zone. We should make it clear, however, that we propose to withdraw our forces whether or not the Russians do the same, except from Berlin where we should remain as long as the Russians do. We should inform them that British and American troops will be withdrawn from the continent of Europe, and we should make clear that the Soviets will not be entitled to the protection of the guarantees in the Ber-

lin Treaty as long as any Russian troops remain West of the Russian frontier.

8. The Federal Republic should undertake an obligation, on the evacuation by the Red Army of the Soviet zone, not to build any fortifications, to destroy existing military airfields and not to station any troops in that zone, provided the Russian forces withdraw behind the Russian frontier, and should register that undertaking with the United Nations. (Alternatively this might take the form of a protocol to the Berlin Treaty.)

9. Finally—and here are the teeth in it—Great Britain and America should attach a joint protocol to their signatures of the Berlin Treaty formally declaring that the "military aid and assistance in their power" under Article 4 will take the form of atomic air power. This protocol, invoking Article 52 of the United Nations Charter, should contain a solemn undertaking that in the event of aggression by any signatory against another (or by any of the three Soviet bloc powers if they do not adhere) the aggressor will instantly be subjected to the full weight of Anglo-American atomic air power. If it is necessary to define aggression (and it would be preferable to leave that open) it should be defined by some simple formula such as that recently suggested by Mr. Bohlen [11]—"crossing the border of another country with armed forces."

Any proposal for the solution of such an intricate problem is bound to be open to criticism, and the foregoing can be criticized on a number of points. But I do not intend to elaborate it in detail, preferring to let it stand in simple

[11] The U.S. Ambassador in Moscow.

form as a basis for discussion, recognizing that it has flaws but attempting neither to expose nor excuse them. I will only comment on two points of some importance. First, it may be asked why this is likely to put fewer difficulties in the way of German reunification than any other proposal, including the E.D.C. To that I think the answer is that no one can say for certain that these tactics will result in evicting the Russians from Eastern Germany and making possible really free elections in a reunified *Reich*; they certainly will not do so in the twinkling of an eye—it may be a wearisome business and we shall need all our patience anyway, but no more so, and indeed I think less, than if we adopt any other scheme that I have heard of—if only because in this respect all other schemes seem to me to amount merely to hoping for the best. The effect of these tactics would be primarily psychological. I think they would at least make it materially more difficult for the Soviets to keep their Polish and Czech subjects in tame subjection and might well bring pressure to bear on Moscow from Warsaw and Prague. Incidentally this scheme would also provide a reasonable safeguard against the new war that the French fear may arise from the Potsdam frontier question. Above all surely it contains the advantages of the initiative. And it does not seem unreasonable to think that the Russians would find it increasingly difficult to maintain their position in the Soviet zone, while the Eastern Germans watch the Allied troops withdrawing from Western Germany and complete sovereign freedom returning to the Federal Republic. In short, I believe this scheme is more likely than others to lead to German reunification within a reasonable time on something like Dr. Adenauer's terms. I can at least say, with Bruce Bairnsfather, "If you know of a better 'ole, go to it."

Finally, there will probably be some who object to the special position proposed for Britain and America in relation to the suggested Berlin Treaty, who will assert that no British or American government would in fact face up to the action proposed when the time came, and anyway that it would be inhumane and morally wrong and inconsistent with the ideals of the United Nations and even of the Brussels Treaty with its references to "fundamental human rights and the dignity of the human person" and all that sort of thing. To them I would reply that all war is an affront to the dignity of the human person; that the primary object of this proposal is to *prevent* war, which, if it happens, will inevitably involve the use of weapons of mass destruction from the air; that if war becomes imminent, to refrain from responsible action and shrink from the prospect even of having to strike the first atomic blow, would not avert war but only make it more certain. "The principal countries of the world . . . have given a special place to the air arm in the scheme designed for the prevention of war." [12] Article 45 of the United Nations Charter provides that "members shall hold immediately available national air force contingents for combined international enforcement action." And the fact that the United Nations Organization is precluded by its own immaturity and present ineptitude from assuming, through its political and military agencies, the control of these air contingents which is envisaged in Article 45, should not paralyze the arm of those members of the United Nations who have the necessary air contingents available and are prepared to use them in a manner "consistent with the pur-

[12] The great authority on international law and usage in relation to air power, Mr. J. M. Spaight, *Air Power Can Disarm*, Pitman, 1948, p. 163.

poses and principles of the United Nations" (Article 52). It is vain to grumble about the special position of Great Britain and the United States—it is one of the facts of life. We *have* a special position in that we are the only powers in N.A.T.O. capable of wielding true air power, and to refuse to accept or use that position to prevent or resist aggression would be a shameful abdication of a moral responsibility.

As to its being inhumane, that is one of the oldest and most constantly disproved accusations against air power. I do not envisage the Anglo-American bomber force taking off at a moment's notice to slaughter millions of innocent civilians by dropping atomic or hydrogen bombs on their cities. If a situation reaches the point when aggression appears so imminent as to call for the application of air power under the "Berlin guarantee," there is still an intermediate step, still a chance of arresting it and saving the peace. I should say here that I am not and never have been a believer in this "bolt from the blue" idea, the sudden, unexpected blow out of a clear sky. Many Americans have the words "Pearl Harbor" graved on their hearts. But Pearl Harbor was not really a bolt from the blue, or should not have been if the U.S. authorities had read the signs aright and taken elementary precautions. There will be again as there have always been an obvious deterioration in the international situation, a mounting tension and indications from Intelligence sources of something cooking. And in these circumstances the procedure I have in mind is that of which the prototype on a diminutive scale was the method known as air control, which the R.A.F. exercised humanely and effectively for years in undeveloped territories like Iraq and the Northwest frontier of India between the wars.[13] The *Operations Manual* of the R.A.F. described the object of air control operations as follows: "to interrupt the normal life of the enemy people to such an extent that the continuation of hostilities becomes intolerable"—note, to interrupt it, *not* to end it by slaughter. In air control, bombing was invariably preceded by ample warning to the tribesmen to evacuate their villages and get their women and children away into safety; *in no circumstances whatever*, not even during a battle when our own troops were engaged with the enemy, were villages bombed without warning. The United States Air Force took a leaf from our book in Japan in 1944. And I would apply the same principle in implementing the "Berlin guarantee." Thus, in a situation clearly likely to lead to war if it develops unchecked—such as the Nazi pressures on Czechoslovakia, Danzig and Poland before 1939—the first step would be a notification in secret, either through the medium of the "Berlin" Council of Ministers or, if that were impossible, direct through diplomatic channels, that the dispute must be submitted to the United Nations or to the "Berlin" Council and settled by agreement there, and that any attempt at a solution by force will bring the guarantee into operation. If that does not have the desired effect and the situation becomes more critical, then we should order full mobilization (if we had not already done so) and move the bomber force to war stations with every circumstance of publicity, and the people of the potential aggressor country should be given an open warning, by radio and by pamphlets broadcast from the air, telling them clearly what will happen if their government uses force

[13] It was constantly criticized at the time by the more conservative as being inhumane, but is now pretty generally recognized as having been far less so than the traditional military method of "burn and scuttle."

and warning them to evacuate a specified list of cities and other objectives, from which should be selected the first targets for attack should that become necessary. If even that is disregarded and the aggressor crosses a neighbor's border with armed forces, or attacks Britain or America in defiance of the warning, then we must strike, instantly and in overwhelming force. I may be an optimist, but I find it difficult to persuade myself that in the face of this procedure, backed by the atomic and the hydrogen bomb, anyone would in fact persist in a course leading to their use.

There are risks in this of course; we should have to steel ourselves to meet a sudden, treacherous attack at any moment during this procedure. But terrible dangers are implicit in the situation we are considering, and this would be a chance—and a real chance—of preventing the calamity of war, at the eleventh hour. Sir Winston Churchill has put forward the idea of a guarantee on the Locarno model; let us have the vision and moral courage to press that suggestion to the only conclusion that could make it effective.

Rimpton,
20 January 1954.

Postscript

In the weeks that have passed since the foregoing chapters were written, there have been certain developments to which it seems desirable to draw attention before the book goes to press.

First, there has been considerable confusion of thought about the meaning of Mr. Dulles's definition of the "New Look" in American defence policy.[1] In many quarters it has been taken to mean that the reaction of the United States to another situation such as that in Korea in June 1950 would be instant "massive" retaliation against Russia or China with the atomic bomb—it being assumed that these would be the places and the means of the United States' own choosing. But the reaction of the United States and their allies to every enemy move cannot be blue-printed in advance; it must depend on and be determined by the situation at the time and by consideration of the vital interests of the Free World in that situation. There are some forms of aggression to which "massive retaliatory power" would be the appropriate, and should be the instant, reaction. But there seems on the face of it no reason to interpret Mr. Dulles's statement as meaning that *any* move on the part of the enemy should be countered in

[1] Mr. John Foster Dulles's speech in Washington, 12 January 1954: "The way to deter aggression is for the free community to be willing and able to respond vigorously at places and with means of its own choosing. Local defences must be reinforced by the further deterrent of massive retaliatory power.

"The basic decision is to depend primarily upon a great capacity to retaliate instantly."

that way; it would certainly make no sense. He has said that "local defences must be reinforced" by the retaliatory capacity of atomic air power, not *replaced* by it; and there has been no public indication that the fighting capacity of the United States land forces is to be reduced. There are wide fields for economy in the U.S. military establishment before that should become necessary.

Clear thinking on this subject has not been made any easier by the curious statement in the British Statement on Defence 1954 that "as the deterrent [of atomic air power] continues to grow it should have an increasing effect on the cold war by making less likely such adventures on the part of the Communist World as their aggression in Korea." There seems to me no inherent reason why it should do anything of the kind. Indeed, if the growth of atomic air power should lead to a premature and excessive reduction of conventional land and air forces in the sacred name of economy, it will probably have exactly the reverse effect. We have already seen a pointer in that direction as a result of the public expressions of anxiety in the United States lest the despatch of a couple of hundred air mechanics to Indo-China should drag the United States into participation in that struggle. It almost amounted to an open notification to Communist China that, whatever happened, the United States did not propose to get involved in that struggle. And it is doubtful whether Peking would believe that support of the Vietminh by "volunteers" on the Korean model would in fact result in the exercise of massive retaliatory power against China.

We really must beware of the tendency to grasp at panaceas. There is no short cut to victory in this cold war. Atomic air power cannot do everything. Apart from the aberration referred to above, and a failure to grasp the nettle of the proper make and shape of modern navies, the British Defence White Paper strikes just about the right balance. It gives high priority to atomic air power as the primary deterrent, but it faces the prospect of prolonged continuation of the cold war and admits the advantages that the Communists enjoy in waging it; while admitting that expenditure on the Army will tend to decline and accepting as an aim a gradual reduction in its size, it accepts also by implication that the Army is the major instrument of Government policy in meeting our cold-war commitments, and aims at building up a strategic reserve in hand, primarily for that purpose.

As I have already tried to show in this book, we in the West must be prepared to maintain sufficient conventional forces to deal with what are, or should be, limited commitments like Korea and Indo-China by limited methods, without having recourse to the dreadful arbitrament of atomic air power. And we must not shrink from using those forces when and where our vital interests are seriously threatened. It is not a question of whether we use the atomic weapon or not; it is how and where we use it and what we use it for. Thermo-nuclear energy is another matter. But we may use nuclear power in a bomb or shell or warhead of a guided missile tactically, for "conventional" purposes. That is merely to employ one projectile to do what we had to use thousands to do in Korea. It is in an entirely different category to unleashing the terrible fury of atomic air power for strategic purposes.

The Berlin Conference has come and gone. There is general agreement that some useful purpose was served.

It should at least dispose of the fancy which created such confusion of thought and aroused so many false hopes last summer, that Soviet foreign policy has undergone any fundamental modification since Stalin's death. The Russians certainly showed no signs of any immediate intention of abandoning any of their forward outposts in Europe, and the reunification of Germany seems no nearer than it was before. It is all to the good that Soviet policy should have been thus clarified, as long as we do not deduce that it is immutable. Berlin should surely make doubly clear the necessity for the West to take active steps to get the Red Army out of Germany and Austria, and should emphasize the dangers of merely waiting and hoping for the best, leaving Soviet communism indefinitely in control east of the Elbe. It is all very well for wise men in comfortable chairs in London and Washington to say that we must not be in too much of a hurry—must maintain our unity, show the world what unpleasant people the Russians are, and feel our way cautiously towards an ultimate settlement. There are millions of unhappy people in East Berlin and Warsaw, Prague and Budapest who can safely be assumed to take a very different view of the urgency of the matter. We have been feeling our way for about six years now. It is more than three years since we proposed a limited rearmament of Germany. Certainly we must maintain our unity in the face of increasing tendencies to dissension—of which Senator McCarthy is not the least dangerous. But just to "ease tension" and sit back accepting the status quo, hoping for the best, is not the best way of doing it, or of inducing the people of the democracies to go on indefinitely accepting compulsory military service and all the cost and strain of rearmament. It did not need a Berlin Conference to prove that the Russians are unpleasant people—most of us know that. What they do want to know, those unfortunates behind the Iron Curtain, is how long they have got to put up with the heel of those unpleasant people on their necks—and what we propose to do about it.

There are only two alternative ways of freeing Eastern Germany from Russian control. One is to push it out by force, which no one in his right mind would contemplate for a moment; the other is to make it increasingly awkward and dangerous for it to stay there. I am not so simple as to suppose that the plan outlined in Chapter 6 is either easy or free from dangers. It is only the bare bones of a policy which would no doubt require some elaboration and modification to meet the wishes and fears of other members of the Atlantic Community. But it surely has the advantage of being constructively positive and, above all, of taking the initiative. A policy on these general lines would put it up to the Kremlin fair and square; make it even more unmistakably clear than it is now what would happen to them if they attacked us; offer them the same guarantee of their security as we claim for ourselves and our allies; and put on them the onus of remaining in Eastern Germany while we withdraw from the West, and of withholding a measure of security for their Polish and Czech satellites which those people would surely welcome if left to themselves. What the Russians would have to give up is their dream of a Communist Germany dominated by Moscow—which, after Berlin, must surely be appearing to them as an increasingly unattainable ambition. Of course, the Russians would not fall for this plan straight away; it did not need a Berlin Conference to prove that. No one can be certain that to withdraw Allied forces from West Germany would result in the Red Army withdrawing from the East—in fact it certainly would not do so immediately. But I believe that, more than any other plan I have heard suggested, it would make it increasingly difficult and awkward for them to maintain their present positions.

The plan has had its critics, as was natural. They have for the most part rightly fastened upon those features of it which are most vulnerable and difficult. It has been criticized as impossible to reconcile with the European Defence Community. No one can yet say with any assurance that the prospects of E.D.C. have been improved by Berlin—in spite of Molotov's crude efforts to wreck it; indeed the reverse may very well be true. I still find it no easier to believe that, even if the French Assembly ratifies the E.D.C. Treaty, we shall ever see the community with its integrated European army and air force in the form at present proposed. It may well be—and indeed it is surely desirable—that there should be some looser, less "totus porcus" form of European defence association with common general and air staffs and a common supply council, which would stop short of merging (or submerging) the national identities and loyalties of the various contingents. Something on those lines—some adaptation of N.A.T.O. perhaps—could surely be devised to meet most of the desiderata in the present E.D.C. scheme and remove some of its major disadvantages, notably the inability of Great Britain to participate in it. An association on these lines could be covered by the Berlin Treaty plan, and would eliminate one of its difficulties in that it would make it possible for Allied contingents of the European forces— other than German corps and wings—to be withdrawn from German soil in peacetime, while still being available instantly to reinforce the Germans in the event of Russian attack.

The proposal to withdraw the British and American forces from the Continent has, of course, been the subject of serious criticisms of the Berlin Treaty plan. It would admittedly demand a special act of faith on the part of the French, which would have to be matched by the most solemn obligations both by Great Britain and the United States, not only to react in the air against any aggression but to hasten to meet it on the ground. It might be necessary for each of us to maintain a token force to act as the "one British soldier" of old Marshal Joffre [2]—perhaps a brigade group [3]—in a French division and a squadron in a Belgian or Italian wing. Mobilization equipment and weapons for reinforcing divisions and wings could be stored on the Continent and a "fire brigade" plan kept in readiness—and practised in peace—to fly in the personnel in emergency. There seems to me nothing between this and an undertaking to retain British and American army corps and tactical air forces permanently in Germany—which I just do not believe makes practical sense, and doubt if anyone else does. An indefinite commitment, linked with an agreement to consult the French before the withdrawal of any forces, would surely be unsatisfactory and a constant source of uncertainty and food for hostile propaganda. Even if Her Majesty's Government or the present U.S. Administration were willing to commit their successors to any permanent undertaking of this sort for defence against Russia (which is hardly conceivable), they would surely not do so to assure the French against the possible resurgence of aggressive German militarism.

[2] Marshal Joffre, when asked before the 1914 war what British forces he wished to see in France in the event of war with Germany, replied, "One British soldier—and we would take good care to see that he was killed"; the idea being to make sure that Great Britain was really involved by the side of France.

[3] U.S. regimental combat team.

The Air Locarno idea in any form has been condemned as lacking in political realism, in that when it came to the point the British Government certainly and the U.S. Administration probably would refrain from using the nuclear weapon against an aggressor, because of public opinion and the fear of retaliation. If this criticism is valid, then we are lost. What it really means is that all our fine words and all the billions spent by successive British and American Governments on rearmament amount to nothing, because when the time comes we shall be afraid to go to war. This talk of retaliation is based on a fallacy—that there is any chance whatever of another great war being waged without recourse to the nuclear weapon. That I think is the important point that arises out of this criticism—that we merely confuse the issue by talking in this context about "using the nuclear weapon" when what we really mean is "going to war"—the word "war" being used in the sense of total world war. The two things are synonymous in these days. It seems doubtful whether the perfectly sincere people who voice this criticism have thought out what it means. Does it mean that they believe nuclear weapons will not be used at all? If so, Sir Winston Churchill certainly does not agree with them, if his words at the head of Chapter 1 mean anything. Her Majesty's Government are clearly not basing their policy on any such assumption; in the 1954 Defence White Paper they have announced their intention to "build up in the R.A.F. a force of modern bombers capable of using the atomic weapon to the fullest extent," and assume that in another great war "atomic weapons would be used by both sides. It seems likely that such a war would begin with a period of intense atomic attacks." The United States Administration obviously have no doubts about the atomic bomb being used—in fact the "New Look" in their defence policy is entirely based on the assumption that it would be used. And finally there is plenty of inferential evidence that the Soviet Government do not have any doubts about it either.

Or does this criticism mean that we should not use the atomic bomb at the beginning of a war, but should wait for something to happen which will make it manifestly impossible for us to withhold its use any longer—the obvious thing being that the enemy uses it first? Surely if we accept that nuclear weapons are bound to be used sooner or later in a third world war, we should be suicidally crazy to adopt any such policy. To begin with, it would amount to rejecting the golden opportunity of preventing total war by the threat of atomic air power—since nothing could be more fatal than to threaten without the fixed intention to enforce the threat in the last resort. And if that deterrent fails, we then surrender to our enemy the initiative either to use it first, or to overrun our allies and get us into a position, with our backs to the wall and the Red Army on the Channel coast, in which we should have to use the nuclear weapon in desperation—and that would be too late.

The proposal for a warning notice in a period of acute tension when war seems imminent has been criticized on the grounds that in future we could not count upon having the time for anything of the sort—that war would be upon us like a bolt from the blue. I have never subscribed to this theory, even before the strength of N.A.T.O. in Europe had grown to a point where the Russians would have to reinforce their garrisons in Germany before launching an attack. The present situation does, however, afford an added safeguard as Sir Winston Churchill emphasized in the House of Commons on 2 March this year. His words on that occasion are worth quoting, because they seem to me to amount to nothing more nor less than that, in his view, we should in these circumstances issue a warning notice of some kind: "An alert meant that not only could immense precautions be taken for the saving of life from atomic bombing raids, but also, short though the time might be, even only a week or two, final efforts could be made to avert a supreme catastrophe, even by the revelation of the strength which the allied forces possessed in the atomic sphere. An alert period meant not only a sure and substantial minimization of the massacre but an additional hope of averting the conflict itself."

There are those who naturally find it difficult to envisage the British, and perhaps still more the American people, going to war under this "Berlin guarantee" to defend Communist Russia against German aggression. Of course, any such thing sounds unrealistic in the conditions of today. But world conditions change. It is as well to remember that it is only ten years since a cardinal essential of Anglo-American strategic policy was to sustain the resistance of Soviet Russia against Germany. But the real answer to this criticism is that of course neither country would go to war to protect Russia—any more than Britain and France went to war in 1939 to protect Poland. We should have to go to war if Germany attacked Russia because that would be World War III started by German aggression, and if Germany conquered Russia she would then be in a position to dominate the world. And the Germany we are here considering is not the democratic Federal Republic of Dr. Adenauer, but a resurgent militarist Germany that had broken away from N.A.T.O. and its other associations with the West—a Germany of 1939, not of 1954. I believe that to be an exceedingly improbable development, but it is not inconceivable, and that is the only Germany we have to fear. Anyway, this criticism ignores the fact that we should have an obligation under U.N.O. to join in the collective security of the Soviet Union against German attack. Sir Winston Churchill clearly does not agree with it—his Locarno suggestion in the House of Commons on 11 May last year was directly related to Russian security. And as recently as 6 February in Berlin Mr. Eden not only offered to extend the Anglo-Soviet Treaty as a reassurance against German aggression, but expressed his willingness to consider any other ways in which we could help to resolve the Soviet Union's anxiety about its security.

Other doubts have been voiced about the suggested "Berlin guarantee." Would it be brought into force in the event of Western Germans fighting Eastern Germans, or the Russians re-entering Azerbaidzhan? How do we define aggression? What frontiers exactly do we guarantee? And so on. To all this the answer is again, this plan is not suggested as a panacea for all ills or a solution to every possible international disagreement. It is merely the outline of a policy to deal with one particular set of circumstances in one particular place—*an armed attack by one European power upon another in Europe*. It is not a cure for civil war; it has nothing to do with defining frontiers, it is not concerned with the integrity of Persia, it makes no claim to be a blueprint for action in every hypothetical future situation. Do not let us try to extend it more widely or define it too closely. If we adopt it, or something like it, as our policy in Europe, we shall have covered the greater part of the course and can then jump the other fences as we come to them.

Rimpton,
12 March 1954.